Historical Dictionary
of ANGOLA

PHYLLIS M. MARTIN

African Historical Dictionaries,
No. 26

The Scarecrow Press, Inc.
Metuchen, N.J., & London
1980

Library of Congress Cataloging in Publication Data

Martin, Phyllis.
   Historical dictionary of Angola.

   (African historical dictionaries.; 26)
   Bibliography: p.
   Includes index.
   1. Angola--History--Dictionaries. I. Title.
II. Series.
DT611.5.M37   967'.3'00321   80-15662
ISBN 0-8108-1322-X

To

Mary C. Wright

ACKNOWLEDGMENTS

The compilation of this small reference book on Angola has only been possible through the publications of other scholars in the field. Whilst many of their studies are listed in the bibliography, the format of this series precludes footnotes, and their collective contribution is gratefully acknowledged here. I should also like to thank David Amaral, Marcus Bird, Jean Meeh Gosebrink, and Patricia Renn Scanlon for their help with the research; Susan Stryker for her typing expertise; and the African Studies Program of Indiana University for financial assistance.

Phyllis M. Martin

TABLE OF CONTENTS

EDITOR'S FOREWORD

Angola is one of the best-known African countries. It has obtained this dubious honor in what appears to be the only way an African nation can attract much attention ... through years of warfare and strife. It was the site of one of the longest and bitterest struggles for independence against Portugal, under the Salazar regime the most adamant colonial power, which was further strengthened in its will to resist by a large settler population and the wealth of its favorite colony, rich in agriculture, raw materials, and petroleum. Nevertheless, the efforts of two and later three liberation armies and a coup in Lisbon combined to make Angola an independent state.

Yet no matter how well known it seemed, the knowledge proved to be highly inadequate when the three opposing nationalist movements, led by three irreconcilable leaders eager to seize power, fell out. Independence ushered in a civil war that is still not totally over and could break out again. From onlookers, the major powers became supporters and sometimes participants, although all were upstaged by Fidel Castro's decision to send a large military force to support the founders of a People's Republic of Angola. Ignorance of the internal situation would seem to include the African states as well, since the Organization of African Unity failed to bring about true cooperation among the liberation movements during the war against Portugal and failed, more strikingly, when it tried to reconcile them during the civil war.

Thus there is a definite need for a book like this one, the main purpose of which is to provide information. It is free from the clever analyses of power relations and exegeses of ideological stands that all too often have passed for information. Instead, it is most generous in brief sketches of the leading figures and events and descriptions of the major ethnic groups and the nation's resources. It has the hard facts and figures that are so badly needed. More significantly, it remembers that Angola has historical roots reaching back beyond the long period of Portuguese colonization, without an understanding of which it is still impossible to comprehend present events.

Dr. Phyllis Martin, Associate Professor of History at Indiana University, has written an amazingly complete and objective book. It results from research and fieldwork in Angola and Portugal and builds on other articles and books she has written on the subject. In addition to the dictionary proper, the lists of rulers, the table of acronyms, a lengthy chronology, and a comprehensive bibliography make this Historical Dictionary a particularly valuable tool.

Jon Woronoff
Series Editor

NOTE ON ORTHOGRAPHY AND TERMINOLOGY

There is no generally accepted, standardized orthography of Angolan proper names.   Indeed, transliteration from one language to another--Bantu languages to Portuguese, English, and German, and so on--has resulted in considerable confusion and multiple variations in the spelling of a single name, according to the inclinations and conventions followed by different writers.   In this book an attempt has been made where possible to spell Bantu and Portuguese names in a phonetic manner, to aid pronunciation by English-speakers.   For example, Kwanza is preferred to Quanza; Chokwe to Cokwe, Tschokwe, or Quioco; Mushikongo to Muxicongo; Mossamedes to Moçamedes; etc.

The increasingly accepted practice among English-speakers of dropping the Bantu prefixes "ba" and "mu" is followed here.   Thus, the name Kongo is used to denote a person (sing.), people (plural), as well as the kingdom of that name.

Another possible source of confusion is the way the names of African countries and towns have changed since independence.   In general, the name current at the date of the events being discussed is used; for example, Belgian Congo became Congo Léopoldville in 1960, Congo Kinshasa in 1966, and Zaire in 1971.   Where there is possible confusion, the alternative or previous name is given in parentheses.   Table 1 includes the name changes of most of the major Angolan towns since 1975.

ABBREVIATIONS AND ACRONYMS

ALIAZO	Alliance des Ressortissants de Zombo
ALLIAMA	Alliance de Mayombe
AMA	Associação das Mulheres de Angola
AMANGOLA	Amigos do Manifesto Angolano
ANANGOLA	Associação Regional dos Naturais de Angola
ASSOMIZO	Association Mutuelle des Ressortissants de Zombo
ATCAR	Association des Tchokwe du Congo, d'Angola et de Rhodésie
CADA	Companhia Angolana de Agricultura
CAUNC	Comité de Acção da União Nacional de Cabinda
CIR	Centro de Instrução Revolucionária
CONCP	Conferência das Organizações Nacionalistas das Colónias Portuguesas
COTONANG	Companhia do Algodão de Angola
CPA	Conselho do Povo Angolano
CVAAR	Corpo Voluntário Angolano de Assistência aos Refugiados
DIAMANG	Companhia de Diamantes de Angola
DISA	Direcção de Investigação e Segurança de Angola

x

DOM	Departamento de Organização de Massas
DOR	Departamento de Orientação Revolucionária
ELNA	Exército de Libertação Nacional de Angola
EPLA	Exército Popular de Libertação de Angola
FALA	Forças Armadas de Libertação de Angola
FAPLA	Forças Armadas Populares para a Libertação de Angola
FDLA	Frente Democrática de Libertação de Angola
FLEC	Frente para a Libertação do Enclave de Cabinda
FNLA	Frente Nacional de Libertação de Angola
FRAIN	Frente Revolucionária Africana para a Independência Nacional das Colónias Portuguesas
FRELIMO	Frente de Libertação de Moçambique
GRAE	Govêrno Revolucionário de Angola no Exílio
IICA	Instituto de Investigação Científica de Angola
JFNLA	Juventude da FNLA
JMPLA	Juventude do MPLA
JUPA	Juventude da UPA
LA	Liga Africana
LGTA	Liga Geral dos Trabalhadores de Angola
LNA	Liga Nacional Africana
MDIA	Movimento de Defesa dos Interesses de Angola
MFA	Movimento das Forças Armadas
MIA	Movimento para a Independência de Angola

MINA	Movimento de Independência Nacional de Angola
MLA	Movimento de Libertação de Angola
MLEC	Movimento de Libertação do Enclave de Cabinda
MLSTP	Movimento de Libertação de São Tomé e Princípe
MNA	Movimento Nacional Angolano
MPLA	Movimento Popular de Libertação de Angola
NGWIZAKO	Ngwizako Ngwizani a Kongo
NTO-BAKO	Partido Nto-Bako
ODP	Organização de Defesa Popular
OMA	Organização das Mulheres de Angola
PAIGC	Partido Africano da Independência da Guiné e Cabo Verde
PCA	Partido Comunista Angolano
PDA	Partido Democrático Angolano
PIDE	Polícia International de Defesa do Estado
PLUA	Partido da Luta Unida dos Africanos de Angola
PNA	Partido Nacional Africano
RPA	República Popular de Angola
SAM	Serviço de Assistência Médica do MPLA
SARA	Serviço de Assistência aos Refugiados de Angola
SWAPO	South-West Africa Peoples' Organization
UEA	União dos Estudantes Angolanos
UGTA	Union Générale des Travailleurs de l'Angola

UNEA	União Nacional dos Estudantes Angolanos
UNITA	União Nacional para a Independência Total de Angola
UNTA	União Nacional dos Trabalhadores de Angola
UPA	União das Populações de Angola
UPNA	União das Populações do Norte de Angola

CHRONOLOGY OF ANGOLAN HISTORY

Chronology involves precise measurement of time, a concept alien to most African societies south of the Sahara. Any chronology of Angolan history must therefore be based on dates known through European written documents and accounts. It overemphasizes events recorded, and those which involved interaction with Europeans. These might not necessarily be the most important happenings for any given society. The chronology also gives more information on events involving the Kongo and Mbundu, who most interacted with the Portuguese over time; and the more recent the period, the more precise is the dating.

15th c. or before	Development of Kongo kingdom in northern Angola.
1483	First encounter between the Kongo and Portuguese. Diogo Cão's expedition arrives in the Zaire estuary.
1491	<u>Manikongo</u> baptized as João I.
1506	Afonso I becomes <u>manikongo</u>.
c. 1510	Spread of the authority of the <u>ngola a kiluanje</u> among the western Mbundu.
1518	Afonso's son Henrique becomes the first black African bishop in the Catholic church.
1520	First Portuguese mission received at the court of the <u>ngola a kiluanje</u>.
1543	Death of Afonso I.
c. 1560	Imbangala reach the Kwanza River.
1561-65	Paulo Dias de Novais detained at the Ndongo court.

1568	Jaga sack Mbanza Kongo.
1571	Paulo Dias de Novais appointed first donatário of of Angola.
1575	Arrival of Dias's expedition at Luanda Island.
1576	Portuguese settlement on the Luanda mainland.
By 1600	Development of small states among the Ovimbundu.
1604	Portuguese presídio at Cambambe.
c. 1612-22	Imbangala-Portuguese alliance.
1617	Benguela founded.
1617-18	Imbangala and Portuguese forces defeat the ngola a kiluanje.
1624	Nzinga becomes ruler of Matamba.
1620s	Kasanje established by the Imbangala.
1641-48	Dutch occupation of Luanda.
1663	Death of Queen Nzinga.
1665	29 October: Portuguese defeat Kongo at the Battle of Mbwila.
1671	Portuguese attack on Pungo Andongo. Presídio established.
c. 1680	Presídio at Caconda.
1704-06	Antonian Movement in Kongo.
1706	Execution of Beatrice of Kongo.
1759	Ndembu-Portuguese war. Fort built at Nkoje.
1784	Portuguese fort at Cabinda destroyed by the French.
1791	Portuguese fort at Ambriz abandoned.
1830s	Plantation coffee production started.

1834   Abolition of Portuguese royal monopoly on ivory.

1836   December: Export of slaves from Angola made
            illegal.

1840   Mossamedes founded.

1842   July: Abolition of slave trade under Portuguese
            flag.

1843   Lobito founded.

1844   Court of Mixed Commission at Luanda.

1845   Presídio at Huíla.

c. 1850   Beginning of Chokwe expansion.

1855   Ambriz occupied by Portuguese.

1872-73   Ndembu revolt.

1878   Legal prohibition of slavery.

1879   Boers in Angola.

c. 1880-   Rubber boom.
1912

1885,   Humbe revolts.
1891, 1897

1885   Chokwe sack Lunda capital, Mussumba.   Settle-
            ment at Sá da Bandeira established.

1890-91   Bié revolt.   Ndunduma of Bié deported.

1902-04   Bailundu Revolt.

1903   Construction of Benguela railway started.

1904-15   Kwanyama wars against the Portuguese.

1904-05   Lunda revolt.

1907-10   Ndembu revolt.

1909-10   Jinga revolt.

1910   Republic proclaimed in Portugal. Liga Ultramarina founded.

1911   Liga Colonial founded.

1912   Liga Angolana founded.

1912-13 Administrative reorganization of Norton de Matos.

1913   Grêmio Africano founded.

1913-16 Kongo rebellion against forced labor.

1917   Diamang founded.

1917-19 Ndembu revolt.

1919   Liga Africana founded.

1921   Partido Nacional Africano founded. Catete "revolt."
        Administrative reorganization.

1926   May: End of the Republic in Portugal.

1929   Liga Nacional Africana formed. Benguela Railway
        reaches Katanga. ANANGOLA founded.

1931   Movimento Nacionalisto Africano founded.

1933   Colonial Act in Portugal reforms administration.

1951   Portuguese colonies become "Overseas Provinces."

1953   PLUA founded.

1955   Angola Communist Party founded.

1956   December: MPLA founded.

1957   UPNA founded in Léopoldville.

1958   UPNA changes name to UPA. MINA joins MPLA.

1959   PIDE launches attacks on Angolan nationalists.
        Many arrests.

1960   June: Arrest of Neto. Protest demonstration in

Icolo-e-Bengo leads to the death of thirty and wounding of two hundred.
November: Twenty-eight Cabindan nationalists shot in Luanda jail.

1961   January: Cotton workers in Baixa de Cassanje strike against malpractices of COTONANG. Severe reprisals. Hijacking of the "Santa Maria" by Galvão draws international attention to Angola. Roberto takes over leadership of UPA.
February 4: Nationalists' attack on Luanda prison.
March 15: Uprising in northern Angola. UN Security Council debate on Angola.
April: CONCP founded in Casablanca. Portuguese start to increase troops in Angola. UN General Assembly debate on Angola ends in a resolution calling for decolonization.
July: UN Security Council requests Portugal "to immediately suspend the measures of repression in Angola."
September: Assimilado status abolished.
October: MPLA opens headquarters in Léopoldville.

1962   March: Alliance of PDA and UPA in FNLA.
April: Creation of GRAE with headquarters in Léopoldville. New Labor Code prohibits forced labor.
July: Neto flees from Portugal to Léopoldville.
December: First National Conference of MPLA in Léopoldville. Neto appointed President of MPLA.

1963   Military front opened in Cabinda by MPLA. FLEC formed in Pointe-Noire.
July: OAU mission recognizes GRAE. FDLA formed.
November: MPLA expelled from Léopoldville. Opens Brazzaville office.

1964   July: Resignation of Savimbi from FNLA/GRAE.
December: Manifesto of AMANGOLA published.

1965   March: OAU starts funding MPLA operations.

1966   March: UNITA formed inside Angola. Savimbi, President.

1967   Cabinda Gulf Oil in production.

1971   June: OAU formally withdraws recognition from
               GRAE.

1973   December "Eastern Revolt" from MPLA.

1974   April 24:   Military coup in Portugal overthrows
               Caetano government.
            May: "Active Revolt" within MPLA.
            July: Portugal declares it is prepared to give in-
               dependence to its African territories.   Armistice
               between Portugal and the three liberation move-
               ments.   Violence by white settlers in Luanda and
               other towns against Africans.   Beginning of
               "people's power" organizations.   Portugal ap-
               points a five-member military junta to govern
               Angola.
            August: MPLA reconstitutes its guerrilla army as
               FAPLA.   Right of Angola to self-determination
               recognized by Portugal.   Rosa Coutinho forms
               Angola Provisional Government.
            September 12-20:   Inter-Regional Conference of
               MPLA militants in Moxico elects Central Com-
               mittee and Political Bureau.
            October: FNLA opens an office in Luanda.
            November: MPLA delegation in Luanda.   Attempted
               coup by FLEC in Cabinda fails.   More attacks
               by white settlers on Africans, especially in Lu-
               anda.

1975   January 15:   Alvor Agreement.
            January 31:   Transitional Government takes office.
               US "Forty" Committee votes to increase clandes-
               tine support to FNLA.
            February 4:   Neto returns to Luanda.   Chipenda
               faction joins FNLA.
            March: Fighting breaks out between FNLA and
               MPLA in Luanda and northern Angola.
            April 28-May 3:   Fighting between FNLA and
               MPLA in Luanda.
            June 21:   Nakuru Agreement.
            July 9-15:   "Battle for Luanda. "   MPLA ousts
               FNLA and UNITA from the capital.   Airlift of
               Portuguese settlers from Angola begins.
            August: Traffic on the Benguela Railway sus-
               pended.   Portugal suspends Alvor Agreement.

High Commissioner in Luanda takes full control of government.

Mid-September: MPLA forces hold twelve out of sixteen provinces.

October 23: Invasion of Angola by South African regular troops with UNITA and FNLA forces. Advance to threaten Luanda. Cuban instructors in Angola.

November 7: Beginning of "Operation Carlota," airlift of Cuban troops to Angola.

November 11: Angola Independence. MPLA proclaims the People's Republic of Angola.

November 12: FNLA and UNITA announce the formation of a coalition government, the Democratic People's Republic of Angola.

November 24: Nigeria the first African country to recognize the RPA.

Mid-December: South African advance turned back.

December 19: US Senate votes to prohibit further covert aid to FNLA and UNITA.

December 22: Gulf Oil announces suspension of Cabinda operations.

1976   January 5: MPLA and Cuban forces take FNLA headquarters at Uige.

January 27: US House of Representatives confirms Tunney Amendment, which prohibits covert aid to Angolan nationalists.

February 11: RPA admitted as forty-seventh member of the OAU.

February: Portugal recognizes the RPA. Administration Decree outlines new political structures for Angola. Law of State Intervention outlines MPLA policy on economic planning.

March 27: Last South African troops withdraw from Angola.

April: Gulf Oil resumes Cabinda operations.

October: RPA signs a twenty-year "Treaty of Friendship" with the USSR.

December 11: Angola admitted as the 146th member of the UN.

1977   Three-Year Development Plan launched.

January: New currency introduced.

March: Portugal and Angola renew diplomatic relations. Katanga nationalists cross from Angola to attack Zaire.

May 27: Attempted coup led by Nito Alves fails.
August: Diamang nationalized.
December: MPLA First Party Congress. MPLA becomes the Angolan Workers' Party.

1978   Year of Agriculture.
May: Katanga nationalists raid Zaire.
July: New Angola-Zaire agreement.
August: State visit by President Neto to Kinshasa.
October: State visit by President Mobutu to Luanda. FNLA and FLEC banned in Zaire.
November 6: Benguela Railway officially reopened by Zaire and Angola.
December: Major reshuffle in Neto government. Prime Minister and three Deputy Prime Ministers dismissed. Visit of Senator George McGovern to Luanda.

1979   May: UNITA increases level of guerrilla activity.
July: New foreign-investment law provides more advantageous conditions for foreign companies.
September 10: Death of President Agostinho Neto.
September 21: José Eduardo dos Santos succeeds Neto as President of Angola, President of MPLA, and Commander-in-Chief of the Armed Forces.

INTRODUCTION

Lying on the Atlantic coast of West Central Africa between about 5 and 18 degrees south and 12 and 24 degrees east, Angola has as its immediate neighbors Zaire, Zambia, and Namibia. In terms of area, it is the seventh-largest country in Africa; its 481,351 square miles include the enclave of Cabinda, separated from the rest of the country by a strip of Zaire territory, but administered as an integral part of Angola. The sea-coast, well provided with natural harbors, is about 1,000 miles long, and the greatest distance from east to west is about 800 miles.

Land and Resources

The physical features of the country can be defined through its position in the broader topography of southern Africa. The much-used analogy of an upturned saucer to describe the predominant contours of the subcontinent seems particularly apt for the area of Angola. The central, eastern, and southern plateaux cover two-thirds of the total area and maintain heights of 4,000-7,000 feet. The coastal lowlands, the rim of the saucer, vary in width from about 100 miles just south of Luanda to 15 miles in the region of Benguela. Between these two areas, a transition zone, where the land rises to about 1,000-3,500 feet, is marked by deep valleys and a series of escarpments and is at times difficult to traverse, as for example in the hinterland of Benguela and Mossamedes. Only in the north, toward the Zaire basin, does this basic relief pattern become less distinct, as the elevation of the interior plateau is lower.

Although such a large country experiences a variety of microclimates, it can be said in general terms that temperatures tend to decrease from north to south and from west to east, whilst rainfall tends to decrease from north to south. As in

1

most areas of tropical Africa, climatic interest centers on rainfall rather than on temperature. Whereas the mean annual temperature varies only some 12 degrees (F) over the whole country, annual rainfall varies from as little as 2 inches in the hinterland of Mossamedes to 70 inches in the Mayombe area of Cabinda. Considerations of climate, elevation, and vegetation together allow Angola to be divided into four regions.

In the north the characteristic vegetation is tropical savanna --that is, grasslands with scattered trees, which grow most profusely along the river valleys. Only in isolated pockets, such as the interior of Cabinda, is there true equatorial rainforest. From the sixteenth century, when it was introduced from Brazil, manioc has been the staple food of the region; yams, sweet potatoes, and bananas are also common. The palm-tree, which supplies such diverse items as oil for cooking and lighting, wine, building materials, and raffia (once used for sewing and weaving before the manufacture and import of cotton textiles), has for centuries been an important resource. Since the nineteenth century northern Angola has been the principal region for the production of coffee, the main cash crop. Cocoa, cotton, tobacco, sisal, rice, palm-oil, and timber are also exported from the area. The prevalence of tse-tse fly north of the Kwanza river makes cattle-keeping impossible, although smaller domestic animals, such as sheep, goats, pigs, and poultry, can survive.

The rolling savannas of the central plateaux have long been a focal point for settlement, both African and European. Here conditions are most congenial for human habitation-- the soil is fertile, there is reliable rainfall, there are fewer tropical diseases than in the northern and coastal areas, and the mean annual temperature of towns like Huambo and Lubango is in the mid-60s (degrees F). Since there is no tse-tse fly, cattle-herding is an important economic activity. Maize, introduced by the Portuguese from Brazil, overtook millet and sorghum as the staple food, probably in the seventeenth century; other common foodstuffs include peas, beans, wheat, and peanuts. The most-developed agricultural land lies along the Benguela railway. Maize, sisal, tobacco, coffee, and cotton are produced for export.

Moving south, the climate is much influenced by the cold Benguela current, which, flowing northward along the Atlantic coast, militates against rain falling on the land. Conditions

of desert-steppe exist in the southern parts of Cunene and
Cuando-Cubango provinces, where the northern fringes of the
Kalahari desert extend into Angola. Here many of the rivers
are seasonal, drying up and then flooding across broad sandy
plains in the rainy season. Sorghum and millet are grown,
but cattle is the primary economic resource.

A fourth region may be distinguished along the low-lying
coast, where agriculture is much conditioned by rainfall.
Along the Kwanza River and in regions to the north precipita-
tion is sufficient for manioc, palm-oil, sugar, and cotton
production. Luanda and Benguela, for centuries the centers
of Portuguese administration, are situated in one of the least
healthy areas of the country, causing high mortality rates
among the early settlers. In the south a strip of the Namib
desert extends north into Mossamedes province. Arid conditions generally preclude much cultivation except in a few
coastal oases that provide foodstuffs for the fishing ports of
Mossamedes and Porto Alexandre.

Everywhere in Angola the people have traditionally augmented
their basic farming economy with other activities--for example, hunting big game, such as antelope, elephant, and
smaller animals, and gathering wild fruits and vegetables.
Fishing is widespread on rivers and lakes. The cold Benguela current ensures a prodigious quantity of fish along the
coast, especially in southern Angola, where it is dried or
otherwise processed before being transported to the interior
or exported. Other crucial resources, such as iron and salt,
are available in various parts of the country and, together
with the other products mentioned, formed the basis for an
extensive local and regional trade network that existed for
centuries, certainly before Europeans arrived on the coast.
In the twentieth century modern techniques of mining have
made possible the exploitation of the country's rich mineral
deposits, especially iron, diamonds, and, most recently, oil.
All these resources together make Angola potentially one of
Africa's wealthiest countries.

People

Among the largest countries on the African continent, Angola
is also one of the most sparsely populated, with a population
at the last census in 1970 of 5, 673, 046, and an average den-
sity of 11. 8 per square mile. Based on the growth rate for
the decade 1960-70, it is estimated that the population will

approach 7 million by 1980. However, any assessment for 1970, or indeed at the present time, is made problematic by population movements the dimensions of which can only be approximated. For example, during the latter part of Portuguese colonial rule, and in the period of the modern armed liberation struggle, 1961-74, as many as half a million refugees fled across the frontiers to Zaire and Zambia. Many of these people returned in the immediate preindependence period, 1974-76; others did not return; and others, especially in northern Angola, did not remain in the country once the victory of MPLA was ensured. Another problem is to assess accurately the number of white settlers. Estimated at about 330,000 in 1974, as many as 90 percent may have left at the time of independence; some of these are now returning.

The population is also unevenly distributed, the result of environmental and historical factors. As already noted, the central plateau region has traditionally been a prime area for settlement. Thus, in 1970, the four central provinces of Benguela, Huambo, Bié, and Huíla accounted for almost half of the country's population. Fertile regions north of the Kwanza River are also points of population concentration-- some 1.5 million in 1970. In contrast, the southern coastal regions, the semidesert areas of the southwest and southeast, and the rolling savannas of the east, are sparsely populated. Although the population is largely rural (85.1 percent in 1970), Angola has in the last two decades or so shared in a phenomenon common to most Third World countries, the drift of people from the countryside to urban centers. The population of Luanda, the capital, increased 111.68 percent in the decade 1960-70 and is now over half a million. Another striking comment on population distribution is that in 1970 about half of Angola's people were concentrated in about 9 percent of the surface area, that is, in the towns and in the Central Highlands.

Angola's population is commonly divided into subgroups or "ethnic groups" that are generally classified on linguistic and cultural criteria (see map on page 11). Such broad divisions, however, must be treated with care if they are taken to imply an unchanging and homogeneous unit. Perhaps the more dynamic concept of population "clusters" is more appropriate. Within any of the given groups--the Kongo, Ovambo, Ovimbundu, and so on--many smaller divisions exist, and there is a blurring, even of the linguistic lines, in peripheral areas, as for example on the Kongo/Mbundu frontiers, where languages spoken by the Hungu, Ndembu, and Sosso exhibit fea-

tures of both Kikongo and Kimbundu. All of the recognized
major groups are based on a series of interrelationships
that have changed over time. Labels may initially have been
applied by outsiders rather than derived from a sense of
common group identity from within. Thus, for example, the
names Mbundu and Ovimbundu were probably Kongo words
initially applied to the peoples living south of them; and
Nganguela, the most heterogeneous group of all, was origin-
ally an Ovimbundu words for their neighbors, before it was
used by colonial administrators and scholars. On the other
hand, recent developments, such as the growth of communication networks, greater mobility, the migration of labor to
other parts of the country and other areas of central and
southern Africa, and conditions of exile in the period 1961-
74, seem to have aided the cementing of group identities.
The influence of modern politics and the establishment of
three major nationalist parties, FNLA, MPLA, and UNITA,
each with an ethnic base in the Kongo, Mbundu, and Ovimbundu regions, have also tended to develop loyalties where
there were previously much-less-defined ties.

History and Historiography

Up until the last two decades Angolan history was generally
written by the Portuguese and reflected their ethnocentric
concerns. The glorification of empire was a necessary un-
derpinning of the "New State" after 1926, and the recording
of Portugal's achievements, both real and mythical, formed
the core of most histories of Angola. Since the 1960s historians, many of whom are non-Portuguese, have looked
more closely at African aspects of Angolan history. Although
the interaction of African societies with the Portuguese remains a predominant theme, it is also recognized that all
Angolan societies have a rich history of their own, much of
which remains to be written.

Angolan history has mainly been studied through ethnically defined regions. Thus, monographs and articles have dealt
with: the Kongo people of northern Angola; the Mbundu of
the Luanda, Malanje, and Kwanza regions; the Ovimbundu of
the Benguela hinterland and Central Highlands; the Nyaneka,
the Ovambo, and their neighbors in southern Angola; and the
Nganguela and Lunda-Chokwe of eastern Angola. The peoples
that interacted most with the Portuguese from the fifteenth
and sixteenth centuries, the Kongo and Mbundu, and to a
lesser extent the Ovimbundu, have received most attention.

This has in part been due to the nature of the written
sources.

Studies that attempt to periodize Angolan history and to pro-
duce some kind of "national" political history tend to high-
light the interaction of African societies with the Portuguese.
And perhaps this is indeed the single most important theme
in the country's history at least from the sixteenth century,
for many of those who did not have direct contact with Europeans were affected indirectly. This comment is most true
for the period from the late nineteenth century until independence, when colonial occupation became more insistent
and pervasive.

Of the little that is known before the fifteenth century, major
historical themes are the settlement of the area by the Bantu, the development of techniques of agriculture and metal-
lurgy; the expansion of long-distance trading networks and of
regional and occupational specialization in production; and the
growth of large-scale political systems.

The arrival of the Portuguese on the coasts of northern Angola at the end of the fifteenth century and their settlement
at Luanda in 1575 was a landmark in the country's history.
Although the colony of Angola for the next three centuries
was largely confined to a strip of territory that stretched
along the coast from the capital to Benguela and inland for
some 100 miles, the Portuguese presence, and especially
their commercial activities, had far-reaching consequences.
Early dreams of mineral wealth and agricultural enterprises,
of the spread of Christianity and the acculturation of Africans, were quickly dispelled by such factors as lack of resources, disease, and African resistance.   By the end of the
sixteenth century the slave trade had taken over as the main
economic activity of the Portuguese and was indeed the principal reason for the continued existence of their colony.
While some historians stress African initiatives and enterprise and the ongoing importance of local agriculture, trade,
and industry, others argue that from the sixteenth century
many Angolan societies were economically tied to the international trading system and ultimately to a position of dependency, a problem that still dominates Third World economies.

The prohibition of the export of slaves from Luanda by the
Portuguese in 1836 is usually taken as another important
watershed in Angolan history.   Some political and economic
systems that had been built on slave-trade prosperity de-

clined, whilst other entrepreneurs, such as the Chokwe, Ovimbundu, Nyaneka, and Ovambo, responded to and benefited
from nineteenth-century demands for ivory, beeswax, and
rubber. Nearer to the coast, the western Mbundu, who more
than any others were affected by the Portuguese presence
over time, were faced with new pressures as white settlers
arrived to establish coffee and sugar plantations, bringing
problems of land alienation, taxation, and forced labor for
indigenous African societies. In respect to the latter, several studies have shown that 1836 by no means saw the end
of the slave trade, since internal demands for labor in Angola and São Tomé continued unabated. Even after 1878,
when the condition of slavery was legally abolished, attitudes
bred through centuries of slave-trading remained. White
settlers continued to view Angolans as a pool of cheap labor;
for many Africans it was a case of "plus ça change, plus
c'est la même chose. "

In the 1840s and 1850s, under the influence of a more im-
perially minded administration in Lisbon, the Portuguese
started to expand from their small coastal colony. Mossamedes was established as a base for further settlement in
southern Angola; a number of sertanejos moved into the Central Highlands; expeditions were dispatched eastward along the
Kwanza to the Cassanje region; and there were attempts to
occupy some key points in northern Angola, such as Ambriz,
where it seemed Portuguese interests were threatened by the
activities of other European traders. But such efforts were
spasmodic and varied with the resources of the Luanda Gov-
ernor and the prevailing policies in Lisbon. It was not until
the last two decades of the nineteenth century that Portugal,
in the face of competition from other European powers, was
impelled to make good its centuries-old claim to the interior
of the country by dispatching military expeditions and treaty-
makers to negotiate with African authorities. Between the
1880s and 1920s national boundaries were delineated through
border treaties with France, Belgium, Britain, Germany,
and, finally, South Africa.

In dealing with the period of occupation and colonial rule,
historians have now moved beyond the narrow confines of diplomatic and administrative history that charted each military
campaign in the interior and each political trade-off in Europe, to look more closely at African history in the twentieth
century. The effects of land alienation, forced labor, migrant labor, low wages, missionary enterprise, changing patterns of agriculture, rural impoverishment, disease, and the

unrealized expectations of a small educated elite are some
of the problems now being studied.   A myriad of individual
and local responses are also being investigated: from "primary" resistance to the nationalist writings of the assimilados, from labor action to the protest of syncretic churches
and early nationalist political organizations.

In 1961, another landmark in Angolan history, Africans finally launched a major rebellion against the harassment and
oppression of the colonial authorities.   This had been especially marked since the advent to power of António Salazar
and the regime of the New State in 1926, which had cracked
down on nationalist sympathizers, forcing them into exile or
clandestine operations within the country.   At the same time
the government promoted the settlement of poor whites from
Portugal, especially after the Second World War.   These
new immigrants filled many of the jobs that might otherwise
have been taken by Africans.   The development of the country was held back, since Portugal, itself one of the poorest
countries in Europe, did not have the resources to invest in
the colonies.   At the same time the xenophobia of the New
State closed off the option of promoting the investment of
other countries in Angola.   Politically, nationalists saw their
neighbors in Congo, Zaire, and Zambia gain independence,
whilst Portugal, itself a totalitarian regime, remained im-
pervious to international or internal pressures for change.

Following the uprisings of 1961 the years until 1974 were
marked by an intensification of the liberation struggle led by
the three nationalist movements, FNLA, MPLA, and UNITA.
From offices in Brazzaville, Kinshasa, Lubumbashi, and
Lusaka, these organizations aided refugees and directed a
guerrilla struggle inside the country, especially in northern
and eastern Angola.   The Portuguese answered with further
repression of nationalists and dispatched troops to Angola,
as many as 60,000 by 1970.   Only a few minor concessions
were made, which did little to mollify nationalist sentiment.
Portugal also tried to promote development through abandon-
ing the closed-investment policy and opening up the country
to multinational corporations, from Krupp of West Germany
to American Gulf Oil.   All these issues have been the subject of a host of publications, most of which lean heavily to
one side or the other.

At the time of the Portuguese coup in April 1974, when a
group of young left-wing army officers overthrew the totalitarian regime, the guerrilla war was at a stalemate.   Cer-

tainly a large number of Portuguese troops were tied down
in Angola, but the liberation movements could not claim to
have won the war as convincingly as the nationalists in the
other Portuguese colonies of Guinea-Bissau and Mozambique.
This was partly due to the fragmented nature of the struggle
in Angola, where three nationalist organizations competed
with each other, as well as waging the war against Portugal.

The rivalries of FNLA, MPLA, and UNITA were a prime
factor in preventing a peaceful transition to independence in
the period 1974-76. But the pressures from international
forces and their interest in Angola's strategic position in
southern Africa also intensified the conflict. The withdrawal
of American aid from FNLA in December 1975, the continu-
ation of Soviet and Cuban aid to MPLA, the discrediting of
UNITA once it had solicited South African help, and the fact
that MPLA was able to hold on to its traditional power-base
in Luanda, the capital, all contributed to the victory of Agostinho Neto's party. The RPA, which achieved independence
on 11 November 1975, had been recognized by most African
and European states by February 1976.

Since the end of the civil war in March 1976, sometimes
called from MPLA's perspective the Second War of Liberation, the government of Agostinho Neto has started to imple-
ment the Marxist-Leninist principles to which MPLA has always subscribed. The problems are many. Apart from
grappling with new political and administrative structures,
the RPA government must rebuild an economy shattered by
war and by the departure of most Portuguese skilled and
semiskilled labor. It has had to deal with factionalism within its ranks and contain low-level UNITA guerrilla activities
in eastern and southern Angola, whilst threatened by incur-
sions of South African forces, which cross the border from
Namibia. As all these problems are worked out, so they
will continue to absorb historians for years to come.

Provinces and Major Towns

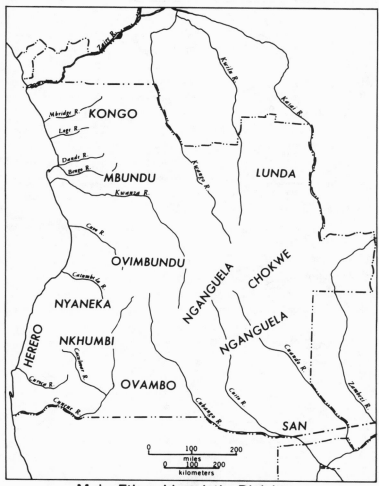

Main Ethno-Linguistic Divisions

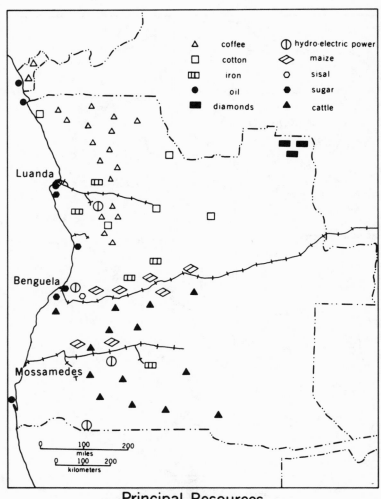

△	coffee	◐	hydro-electric power
□	cotton	◈	maize
⊞	iron	○	sisal
●	oil	●	sugar
■	diamonds	▲	cattle

Luanda

Benguela

Mossamedes

0   100   200
miles
0   100   200
kilometers

Principal Resources

TABLE 1

Name Changes of Angolan Towns Since Independence

Present Name	Previous Name
BAILUNDO	TEIXEIRA DA SILVA
BALOMBO	NORTON DE MATOS
BIBALA	VILA ARRIAGA
BIE	SILVA PORTO
BOCOYO	SOUSA LARA
CAALA	ROBERT WILLIAMS
CAMACUPA	GENERAL MACHADO
CAPELONGO	ARTUR DE PAIVA
CELA	SANTA COMBA
CHIBIA	JOÃO DE ALMEIDA
GANDA	MARIANO MACHADO
HUAMBO	NOVA LISBOA
LUACHIMO	PORTUGALIA
LUAU	TEXEIRA DE SOUSA
LUBANGO	SA DA BANDEIRA
LUENA	LUSO
LUMBALA	GAGO COUTINHO
MBANZA KONGO	SÃO SALVADOR
MENONGUE	SERPA PINTO
MUXALUANDO	GENERAL FREIRE
NDALATANDO	SALAZAR

Table 1 (continued)

Present Name	Previous Name
NGIVA	PEREIRA DE EÇA
NGUNZA	NOVO REDONDO
NZETO	AMBRIZETE
SAURIMO	HENRIQUE DE CARVALHO
SOYO	SANTO ANTONIO DO ZAIRE
UIGE	CARMONA

TABLE 2

Heads of Portuguese Government in Angola

Donatário

1575-1589	Paulo Dias de Novais

Governors

1589-1591	Luís Serrão
1591-1592	André Ferreira Pereira
1592-1593	Francisco de Almeida
1593-1594	Jerónimo de Almeida
1594-1602	João Furtado de Mendonça
1602-1603	João Rodrigues Coutinho
1603-1606	Manuel Cerveira Pereira (1)
1607-1611	Manuel Pereira Forjaz
1611-1615	Bento Banha Cardoso
1615-1617	Manuel Cerveira Pereira (2)
1617-1621	Luís Mendes de Vasconcelos
1621-1623	João Correia de Sousa
1623	Pedro de Sousa Coelho
1623-1624	Simão de Mascarenhas
1624-1630	Fernão de Sousa
1630-1635	Manuel Pereira Coutinho
1635-1639	Francisco de Vasconcelos da Cunha
1639-1645	Pedro César de Meneses

15

Table 2 (continued)

1645-1646	Francisco de Souto-Maior
1646-1648	(junta)
1648-1651	Salvador Correia de Sá e Benevides
1651-1653	Rodrigo de Miranda Henriques
1653-1655	Bartolomeu de Vasconcelos da Cunha
1655-1658	Luís Mendes de Sousa Chicorro
1658-1661	João Fernandes Vieira
1661-1666	André Vidal de Negreíros
1666-1667	Tristão da Cunha
1667-1669	(juntas)
1669-1676	Francisco de Távora
1676-1680	Aires de Saldanha de Sousa e Meneses
1680-1684	João da Silva e Sousa
1684-1688	Luís Lobo da Silva
1688-1691	João de Lencastre
1691-1694	Gonçalo da Costa de Alcácova Carneiro de Meneses
1694-1697	Henrique Jacques de Magalhães
1697-1701	Luís César de Meneses
1701-1703	Bernardino de Távora de Sousa Tavares
1703-1705	(junta)
1705-1709	Lourenço de Almada
1709-1713	António de Saldanha de Albuquerque Castro e Ribafria
1713-1717	João Manuel de Noronha
1717-1722	Henrique de Figueiredo e Alarcão
1722-1725	António de Albuquerque Coelho de Carvalho
1725-1726	José Carvalho da Costa
1726-1732	Paulo Caetano de Albuquerque
1733-1738	Rodrigo César de Meneses
1738-1748	João Jacques de Magalhães

16

1749-1753	António de Almeida Soares Portugal de Alarcão Eça e Melo, Marquês do Lavradio
1753-1758	António Alvares da Cunha
1758-1764	António de Vasconcelos
1764-1772	Francisco Inocêncio de Sousa Coutinho
1772-1779	António de Lencastre
1779-1782	João Gonçalo da Câmara
1782-1784	(juntas)
1784-1790	José de Almeida e Vasconcelos Soveral Carvalho e Albergaria, Barão de Moçâmedes
1790-1797	Manuel de Almeida Vasconcelos
1797-1802	Miguel António de Melo
1802-1806	Fernando António de Noronha
1807-1810	António de Saldanha da Gama
1810-1816	José de Oliveira Barbosa
1816-1819	Luís da Mota Fêo e Torres
1819-1821	Manuel Vieira Tovar de Albuquerque
1821-1822	Joaquim Inácio de Lima
1822-1823	(junta)
1823	Cristóvão Avelino Dias
1824-1829	Nicolau de Abreu Castelo Branco
1829-1834	José Maria de Sousa Macedo Almeida e Vasconcelos, Barão de Santa Comba Dão
1834-1836	(junta)
1836	Domingos de Saldanha de Oliveira Daun

Governors-General

1837-1839	Manuel Bernardo Vidal
1839	António Manuel de Noronha
1839-1842	Manuel Eleutério Malheiro
1842-1843	José Xavier Bressane Leite
1844-1845	Lourenço Germack Possolo
1845-1848	Pedro Alexandrino da Cunha

Table 2 (continued)

1848-1851	Adrião da Silveira Pinto
1851-1853	António Sérgio de Sousa
1853	António Ricardo Graça
1853-1854	Miguel Ximenes Rodrigues Sandoval de Castro e Viegas, Visconde de Pinheiro
1854-1860	José Rodrigues Coelho do Amaral (1)
1860-1861	Carlos Augusto Franco
1861-1862	Sebastião Lopes de Calheiros e Meneses
1862-1865	José Baptista de Andrade (1)
1866-1868	Francisco António Gonçalves Cardoso
1869-1870	José Rodrigues Coelho do Amaral (2)
1870-1873	José Maria da Ponte e Horta
1873-1876	José Baptista de Andrade (2)
1876-1878	Caetano Alexandre de Almeida e Albuquerque
1878-1880	Vasco Guedes de Carvalho e Meneses
1880-1882	António Eleutério Dantas
1882-1886	Francisco Joaquim Ferreira do Amaral
1886-1891	Guilherme Augusto de Brito Capelo (1)
1891-1893	Jaime Lôbo Brito Godins
1893-1896	Alvaro da Costa Ferreira
1896-1897	Guilherme Augusto de Brito Capelo (2)
1897-1900	António Duarte Ramada Curto (1)
1900-1903	Francisco Xavier Cabral de Oliveira Moncada
1903-1904	Eduardo Augusto Ferreira da Costa (1)
1904	Custódio Miguel de Borja
1904-1906	António Duarte Ramada Curto (2)
1906-1907	Eduardo Augusto Ferreira da Costa (2)
1907-1909	Henrique Mitchel de Paiva Couceiro
1909	Alvaro António da Costa Ferreira
1909-1910	José Augusto Alves Roçadas
1910-1911	Caetano Francisco Claúdio Eugénio Gonçalves

1911-1912	Manuel Maria Coelho
1912-1915	José Mendes Ribeiro Norton de Matos (1)
1915-1916	António Júlio da Costa Pereira de Eça
1916-1917	Pedro Francisco Massano do Amorim
1917-1918	Jaime Alberto de Castro Morais
1918-1919	Filomeno da Câmara Melo Cabral (1)
1919-1920	Francisco Carlos do Amaral Reis

Governors-General/High Commissioners

1921-1924	José Mendes Ribeiro Norton de Matos (2)
1924	João Augusto Crispiniano Soares
1924-1925	Antero Tavares de Carvalho
1925-1926	Francisco Cunha Rêgo Chaves
1926-1928	António Vicente Ferreira
1928-1929	António Damas Mora
1929-1930	Filomeno da Câmara Melo Cabral (2)
1930-1931	José Dionísio Carneiro Sousa Faro
1931-1934	Eduardo Ferreira Viana
1934-1935	Júlio Garcês Lencastre
1935-1939	António Lopes Mateus
1939-1941	Manuel da Cunha e Costa Marquês Mano
1941-1942	Abel de Abreu Souto-Maior
1942-1943	Alvaro de Freitas Morna
1943	Manuel Pereira Figueira
1943-1947	Vasco Lopes Alves
1947	Fernando Falcão Pacheco Mena
1947-1955	José Agapito da Silva Carvalho
1956-1959	Horácio de Sá Viana Rebêlo
1960-1961	Alvaro Rodrigues da Silva Tavares
1961-1962	Venâncio Augusto Deslandes
1962-1966	Silvino Silvério Marquês (1)
1966-1972	Camilo Augusto de Miranda Rebocho Vaz

Table 2 (continued)

1972-1974	Fernando Augusto Santos e Castro
1974 (June-July)	Silvino Silvério Marquês (2)
1974 (July)-1975 (Jan.)	António Rosa Coutinho (successively, President of Military Junta; President of Provisional Government; Acting High Commissioner)
1975 (Jan.-Aug.)	António Silva Cardoso (High Commissioner)
1975 (Aug.)	Ernesto Ferreira de Macedo (interim High Commissioner)
1975 (Aug.-Nov.)	Leonel Alexandre Gomes Cardoso (High Commissioner)

Sources: Henige, David P. Colonial Governors from the Fifteenth Century to the Present. Madison: Wisconsin University Press, 1970, pp. 231-233.

Africa Contemporary Record.

Facts and Reports.

20

TABLE 3

Angolan Population Estimates in the Twentieth Century

Year	Total Population	Density Per Square Km.	Real Growth	Growth Rate
1900	2, 716, 000	2. 17	--	--
1910	2, 921, 500	2. 34	205, 500	7. 56%
1920	3, 131, 200	2. 51	209, 700	7. 18%
1930	3, 343, 500	2. 68	232, 300	6. 78%
1940	3, 738, 010	2. 99	394, 510	11. 79%
1950	4, 145, 266	3. 32	407, 256	10. 55%
1960	4, 840, 719	3. 88	695, 453	16. 78%
1970	5, 673, 046	4. 55	832, 327	17. 19%

Note: 1940-70 figures based on Census returns. The figures for other years are estimates.

Sources: Informações Estatísticas. Luanda: Direcção Provincial dos Serviços de Estatística, 1972.

Actualidade Económica. Luanda. Vol. I, No. 8, (December 1974).

TABLE 4

Population of Angola, According to Districts
(1970 estimates)

Districts	Population
Cabinda	80, 857
Zaire	41, 766
Uige	386, 037
Luanda	560, 589
North Kwanza	298, 062
South Kwanza	458, 592
Malanje	558, 630
Lunda	302, 538
Benguela	474, 897
Huambo	837, 627
Bié	650, 337
Moxico	213, 119
Cuando-Cubango	112, 073
Mossamedes	53, 058
Huíla	644, 864
TOTAL	5, 673, 046

Source: 1970 Census, Direcção Provincial dos
Serviços de Estatística, 1972.

TABLE 5

Foreign Trade, 1965-74
(million escudos)

Year	Exports	Imports	Balance
1965	5, 747	5, 601	+ 146
1966	6, 359	5, 948	+ 411
1967	6, 838	7, 909	- 1, 071
1968	7, 788	8, 710	- 922
1969	9, 387	9, 261	+ 126
1970	12, 172	10, 595	+ 1, 577
1971	12, 147	12, 128	+ 19
1972	13, 923	10, 728	+ 3, 195
1973	19, 158	13, 269	+ 5, 889
1974	30, 996	15, 836	+15, 160

Sources: Banco de Angola, Annual Report 1973.

Economic Intelligence Unit, Mozambique and Angola, Annual Supplement, 1975 and 1976.

Actualidade Económica, Luanda, Vol. I, No. 8, (December 1974).

TABLE 6

Principal Products Exported, 1970-74
(million escudos)

Product	1970	1971	1972	1973	1974
Coffee	3, 880	4, 026	3, 835	5, 090	6, 274
Diamonds	2, 340	1, 523	1, 583	2, 000	2, 463
Iron Ore	1, 426	1, 187	1, 012	1, 211	1, 212
Crude Oil	1, 397	2, 157	3, 535	5, 756	14, 975
Cotton	421	649	284	620	469
Maize	315	182	143	250	189
Fish Meal	289	212	531	740	487
Sisal	238	222	339	468	1, 271
Bananas	118	175	264	313	290

Sources: Banco de Angola, Annual Report 1971-1973.

Economic Intelligence Unit, Mozambique and Angola, Annual Supplement, 1975.

THE DICTIONARY

-A-

"ACTIVE REVOLT" (Revolta Activa). An opposition group within MPLA that was formed in Brazzaville in May 1974. Led by left-wing intellectuals, some of whom, like the brothers Mário Coelho Pinto de Andrade and Joaquim Pinto de Andrade, had played important roles in the early development of the party, the "Active Revolt" probably never rallied more than about seventy supporters. Critical of MPLA's military and political weakness at the time, the group in particular attacked Neto for his leadership, accusing him of "presidentialism" and secrecy. Seven leaders of the group were arrested in April 1976 by the MPLA government.

ADMINISTRATION.
    1) COLONIAL. From the sixteenth century the chief Portuguese representative in Angola was the Governor, who ruled Luanda and the interior through subordinate officials, usually military officers. The pattern of early Portuguese administration developed in the seventeenth and eighteenth centuries through a line of fortresses called presídios along the Kwanza valley and at key points to the north and south. These were the centers of administrative-military areas. By the mid-nineteenth century other units, distritos, often based on towns, were also recognized. The officials in charge of these local administrative points were variously called chefes, regentes, and capitães-mores. Lack of money and manpower as well as African resistance meant that the Portuguese administration was frequently tenuous in the interior, even in the nineteenth century, outside the forts. Crucial to their continuing influence were African chiefs, sobas, who were recognized by the Luanda government in return for taxes and services, such as providing porters and soldiers, and procuring food, slaves, and other trade goods.

25

Between 1885 and 1926 the political boundaries of modern Angola were defined through treaties with France, Belgium, Britain, Germany, and South Africa. African wars of resistance continued throughout this period.

In the twentieth century the administrative relationship between the colony of Angola and the metropole varied according to the prevailing philosophies and strategies of the Lisbon government. At times the Luanda administration enjoyed almost complete autonomy (for example, in 1921, when the Governor-General's title was changed to High Commissioner in recognition of his wide-ranging authority); at other times it was much more constricted in its power (for example, after 1930 with the colonial policy of the "New State"). Administrative divisions within Angola were also restructured on several occasions.

In the latter part of the colonial period the administrative system was based on the Overseas Administrative Reform law of 1933 and modifications thereafter. Overall responsibility was vested in the Prime Minister and Council of Ministers in Lisbon, and in the Overseas Ministry, which retained ultimate power in all essential matters relating to Angola. Some degree of fiscal autonomy and administrative decentralization meant that considerable powers rested with the Governor-General in Luanda. Usually a military officer, the latter was appointed for a four-year term by the Overseas Ministry. In the tradition of the metropole there was a strong executive government, the Governor-General ruling with six secretaries, and a weak Legislative Council that met for three months in the year. Angola was divided into districts (distritos), which numbered sixteen at the time of independence. Districts were subdivided into concelhos (townships) and circunscrições (for rural areas). Further administrative subdivisions included parishes (freguesias) and administrative posts (postos administrativos), the latter being administered by a chefe do posto, a key figure in the system of local government. In the administrative posts African villages were grouped together under regedores and sobas.

In 1951 the status of Angola together with that of Portugal's other African territories was changed from that of a Colony to that of an Overseas Province. This was an attempt to symbolize the integration of the colonies with the metropole and thus to resist increasing international pressures for decolonization.

2) SINCE INDEPENDENCE. The constitution of the

RPA and a law of February 1976 set out the principles
on which the administration is based. An essential concept is that of "people's power, " that is, the effective
participation of the masses in the government of the
country. The system provides for a pyramid-shaped
structure with each level a step to the one above. In
local areas the process starts with mass meetings that
elect Village (povoações) Committees in rural areas and
Neighborhood (bairros) Committees in urban areas.
These local committees merge at the level of Communes
(comunas). Municipal councils (concelhos) and the Provincial (províncias) Committees are the next upward
steps. The supreme popular body is the People's Assembly; however, this has not yet been organized, either
in its composition or manner of election. In fact, due
to the wartime conditions of the immediate postindependence period and the many tasks of national reconstruc-
tion, the details of the administrative system outlined
above are not yet in operation in all areas.

    The administration of Angola is very closely tied
to MPLA; this is seen in the constitutional provisions
for top levels of government. The President of the Republic is also the President of MPLA and presides over
the Council of the Revolution, which will remain the
supreme legislative and executive authority until the
People's Assembly is organized. The Council of the
Revolution is composed of the Political Bureau of MPLA,
the FAPLA General Staff, the Provincial Commissioners,
the Political Commissioners of the Military Fronts, and
government members appointed by the party. The Provincial Commissioners are appointed by the Council of
the Revolution on the recommendation of MPLA. The
party also appoints delegates to the various committees
of local government. See PRESIDIOS; CAPITÃO-MOR;
SOBA; BAIRRO; "PEOPLE'S POWER"; MPLA.

AFONSO I. Manikongo (ruler of Kongo) from 1506 to 1543,
    Afonso I promoted Christian and European influence in
    his kingdom, welcoming missionaries and technical aid
    from Portugal, whilst sending several of his younger
    relations for education in Europe. How genuine his con-
    version, or how far he saw the creation of a literate
    Europeanized class in Kongo as a means of consolidating
    his own power, is not clear. His relations with Portu-
    gal started to break down over the activities of slave-
    traders, especially those from São Tomé, whom neither
    he nor the Lisbon court could control.

ALDEAMENTOS. Strategic resettlement villages organized
by the Angolan government in the 1960s, especially in
eastern Angola, as guerrilla insurgency grew. Previously dispersed groups of Africans were grouped together
in settlements that aimed both to provide security against
attack and to prevent nationalist insurgency among local
populations.

ALLIANCE DES RESSORTISSANTS DE ZOMBO (ALIAZO).
The Zombo, a Kongo subgroup, formed ALIAZO from
the previous ASSOMIZO in 1959. ALIAZO was nonvio-
lent and conciliatory, which reflected the views of its
Christian, middle-class leaders and supported Zombo
autonomy within an Angolan federation. In 1961 it
changed its name to the Partido Democrático de Angola
(PDA) to try to broaden its base, and in 1962 joined
with the UPA in the united front, GRAE.

ALVES, NITO. Born about 1945, a Mbundu, from Piri in
N. Kwanza district, Alves studied at the Protestant
school in Piri, and also in Malanje and Luanda. He was
employed in the Department of Finance in Luanda, but
in 1966 his nationalist activities forced him to flee from
PIDE into the Dembos region. Here he worked with other MPLA guerrillas and in 1973 was appointed Political
Commissar for the First Military Region. He was
elected to the MPLA Central Committee at the party Regional Conference in Moxico in September 1974. In November 1975 he was appointed by Neto to be Minister of
Interior in his first government.
      In Luanda, Nito Alves, who had thus come up
through the MPLA ranks, became the hero of the masses
and a focus for those who supported "people's power."
An orator and crowd-pleaser, he was seen as a spokesperson for the black population against the mestiço, intellectual MPLA leadership, and his power increased as
the masses became disillusioned with the food shortages
and other hardships of the postindependence period.
      In the fall of 1976 he lost his job as Minister of
Interior, and on 21 May 1977 he was expelled from the
Central Committee of MPLA, charged with "factionalism." Accused of planning the abortive coup of 27 May
1977, he fled to the Dembos region, where he was captured in July 1977.

ALVOR AGREEMENT. Signed on 15 January 1975, between
representatives of Portugal, FNLA, MPLA, and UNITA,

at Alvor, Algarve, Portugal, this agreement set down
the basic principles of government for Angola in the
transitional period leading to independence.

The major provisions set the date for independence, affirmed the integrity of Angola including Cabinda,
determined the composition and powers of the Transitional Government, and agreed on a general cease-fire.
Portugal suspended the Agreement in August 1975 after
the outbreak of civil war between the liberation movements had made its provisions unworkable.   See TRANSI-
TIONAL GOVERNMENT.

AMBAKISTAS.   Name derived from the settlement at Mbaka
(Ambaka), some 170 miles east of Luanda, where the
Portuguese established a fort in 1618.   Around this
point there developed in the seventeenth and eighteenth
centuries a Luso-Mbundu community who spoke and
sometimes wrote Portuguese, who supplied the Portuguese with trade goods, such as slaves and ivory, and
who in general promoted Portuguese advance in the interior.   By the mid-nineteenth century the name ambakistas was in common use to refer to this group of people.   The Ambakista dialect of Kimbundu spread as a
trade language and is now widely spoken among the eastern Mbundu.

AMBRIZ.   A small coastal town in northwest Angola with a
good anchorage but little developed as a port.   By the
late eighteenth century Ambriz was a growing slave entrepôt frequented by French and English ships.   The
Portuguese tried to counteract the threat to their own
trade at Luanda by building a fort there in 1790; this
was abandoned the next year.   Ambriz was again occupied by the Portuguese in 1855, when they wanted to im-
pose customs duties on the rubber, ivory, and palm-oil
trade.   It was also used as a base from which to send
military expeditions into the Kongo area in the late nineteenth and early twentieth centuries.

AMIGOS DO MANIFESTO ANGOLANO (AMANGOLA).   A group
of twenty-four predominantly Ovimbundu nationalists,
many of whom had defected from the UPA/GRAE.   The
group, which included several of the future UNITA leaders, such as Savimbi and Kalundungo, issued a manifesto
in December 1964 calling upon exiled Angolans to move
back inside their country and mobilize the people for
guerrilla warfare.   See UNITA.

ANDRADE, JOAQUIM PINTO DE.   Priest and nationalist
leader.   Born 22 July 1926 in Golungo Alto, N. Kwanza
region, he attended a seminary in Luanda and the Greg-
orian University in Rome.   This was followed by parish
work in Luanda, where he became Chancellor of the
archdiocese.
        Father Andrade was an early supporter of MPLA,
and in 1960 he was arrested along with Neto and other
nationalist leaders in Luanda.   Then began fourteen years
of exile and political persecution, spent partly in prison
in Lisbon and partly under house arrest in a Benedictine
monastery in Porto.   In 1962, in his absence, Joaquim
Andrade was chosen as "honorary president" of MPLA
at a conference in Léopoldville.
        Released from detention in 1974, Andrade together
with his younger brother, Mário, quickly found himself
at odds with the party leadership and formed the opposition "Active Revolt" group.   He was imprisoned by the
Neto administration in April 1976, but later released.

ANDRADE, MARIO COELHO PINTO DE.   Poet, literary crit-
ic, and nationalist leader.   Born 21 August 1928 in Golungo Alto, N. Kwanza region, he attended secondary
school in Luanda before leaving for Lisbon in 1948 to
study philology.   In the Portuguese capital and later in
Paris, where he went to study sociology in the Sorbonne
in 1954, Andrade came into contact with other future African nationalist leaders, such as Neto and Cabral.   In
Paris he joined the growing literary circle of African and
Caribbean writers, became secretary of the journal Présence Africaine, and helped to organize the Second Congress of Negro Writers and Artists.
        A founding member of MPLA, Andrade became
President of the movement 1960-62, handing the reins
over to Neto when the latter escaped from Portugal.
Thereafter, Andrade was party Secretary for Foreign Affairs for a short time, helping to establish the Liberation
Army of MPLA.   He was also active in the CONCP.
Differences with Neto surfaced briefly in 1963 and again
in April 1974, when with his older brother, Joaquim
Andrade, he joined the "Active Revolt" group.
        One of Angola's leading intellectuals, Mário de
Andrade, a sophisticated and cosmopolitan figure, helped
to establish MPLA's positive intellectual image in European literary circles.   His poetry and articles have been
widely published, especially in Présence Africaine.   He
has published a number of anthologies of poetry introduc-

ing and interpreting lusophone African writing to the international audience.

ANTONIAN MOVEMENT. A Kongo Christian sect founded
about 1704 by a young woman named Beatrice, who
claimed to be the reincarnation of Anthony of Padua, a
saint whose cult had been introduced to the Kongo in the
mid-seventeenth century. See BEATRICE OF KONGO.

ANTONIO, MARIO (FERNANDES DE OLIVEIRA). Born 5
April 1934 in Maquela do Zombo, Mário António, a Luso-
African poet and short-story writer, attended school in
Luanda. He was one of the outstanding talents in a literary movement that tried to create an authentic Angolan
literature in the period 1951-62, publishing in the re-
views Mensagem and Cultura. Since the mid-1960s he
has lived in Portugal, where he is an administrator at
the Gulbenkian Foundation.

ARMED FORCES.
          1) COLONIAL. The colonial army from the six-
teenth century until about 1930 consisted of two main
forces. The "first-line" army was composed of European troops and rarely numbered more than about 2,000.
The "second-line" army, the guerra preta, consisted of
African soldiers and formed the backbone of the colonial
army. Sometimes forcibly conscripted, this force was
raised by sobas or on a more regular basis by the Portuguese with wages and uniforms. After about 1930 the
guerra preta was incorporated into "native companies"
with Portuguese sergeants and officers.
          After 1961 and during the period of nationalist in-
surgency, there was a massive buildup of the army in
Angola. In 1961 the armed forces numbered about 9,000,
of which about 2,000-3,000 were European. By 1966
the army numbered about 50,000. For 1973-74 estimates
range from about 60,000-70,000. Official Portuguese
figures claim 60 percent of these were African, but this
estimate most likely included all forces, such as para-
military and specially trained groups; the proportion of
Africans in regular army units may have been as low as
35 percent.
          2) SINCE INDEPENDENCE. During the Wars of
Liberation, 1961-74, and in the ensuing armed struggle
between the three nationalist movements, 1974-76, FNLA,
MPLA, and UNITA each organized, armed, and trained
their own forces. In the constitution of the RPA, the

MPLA army, FAPLA, was institutionalized as the national army. Every Angolan citizen between the ages of eighteen and thirty-five, regardless of sex, religion, degree of literacy, and ethnic origins, is liable to twenty-four months military service. After this time they are placed in the Reserves.

An important adjunct to FAPLA is the People's Defence Organization, a people's militia that can be called out to maintain the peace internally and to defend the territorial integrity of Angola. ODP members receive military, political, and ideological training and are organized on the basis of local cells, several cells uniting in a sector, sectors in zones, and zones in regions.

ASSIMILADO. A term used loosely to mean an "assimilated" person, an African or mestiço who could speak and write Portuguese, and who had adopted Portuguese cultural values.

Following legislative measures of the 1920s the term took on a more specific legal meaning. At this time Africans in Portuguese colonies were designated as a separate legal category called indígenas. In order to escape this status, and to be eligible for the privileges that Portuguese citizens enjoyed, nonwhites, both Africans and mestiços, had to prove that they had become "assimilated." In order to be recognized as an assimilado, a person had to be over eighteen, speak Portuguese fluently, show ability to support oneself and one's family, adopt Portuguese cultural values, and be of good character. The weakness of the education system was a prime reason for the failure of the policy, and by 1960 only about 80,000 were counted as não-indígena or assimilado, compared with 4.5 million indígenas. After the rebellion of 1961 Portugal abandoned the policy, and all who lived in the Overseas Territories were said, theoretically, to have the same constitutional and legal rights. See INDIGENA.

ASSIS, ANTONIO DE, JUNIOR. 1878-1960. Journalist, novelist, lawyer. An ambakista, mestiço, and assimilado, Assís Júnior qualified as a lawyer and worked his way up in the colonial civil service. An early nationalist leader associated with the Liga Angolana, he was imprisoned in 1917 on conspiracy charges by the Portuguese whilst protesting African land alienation and forced labor in N. Kwanza region. Released, he was impris-

oned a second time in 1921.   A few years later he
ceased to be an active nationalist.

His writings included a two-volume work giving
the background to the 1917-18 incidents and his hopes for
Angola's future.   He also showed his identification with
indigenous culture in his famous novel O Segredo da
Morta (The Dead Woman's Secret), published in 1934,
and in a Kimbundu-Portuguese dictionary published in the
1940s.

ASSOCIATION MUTUELLE DES RESSORTISSANTS DE ZOMBO
(ASSOMIZO).   A Zombo ethnic mutual-aid society founded
in Léopoldville in 1956 by members of the Zombo emigré
community.   In 1959, after UPA refused to sanction a
merger, the Zombo community decided to compete by
transforming itself into a political party, ALIAZO.   See
ALIAZO.

-B-

BAILUNDU.   An important state of the Ovimbundu, Bailundu
was bordered by its chief rivals, Bié to the east and
Wambu to the south, and like Bié established trading contacts with the Portuguese at Benguela.   The expansion of
the rubber trade in the 1890s and the weakness of Bié
due to the advance of Portuguese farmers and traders
allowed Bailundu to emerge as the most important Ovimbundu state at the end of the nineteenth century.   The
Bailundu are particularly noted for their determined resistance to Portuguese expansion in the area at the beginning of the twentieth century.   The "Bailundu Revolt,"
1902-04, drew support from other neighboring Ovimbundu
and non-Ovimbundu, and was only ended when the Portuguese sent a military expedition into the Central Highlands.   It became a favorite region in Angola for white
settlement.   See OVIMBUNDU.

BAIRRO.   A section or quarter of a city.   The Comissão do
Bairro (Neighborhood Committee) is a key unit of local
government in urban areas under the Angolan constitution.
The Neighborhood Committees have a mandate from
MPLA in the immediate postindependence period to organize the life of the neighborhood and provide essential
social services, such as food cooperatives, schools,
clinics, information services, and so on.

BANKING.   In November 1976, on the first anniversary of
    Angola's independence, the government announced the na-
    tionalization of the country's two major banks: Banco
    de Angola, the central issuing bank, and Banco Comer-
    cial de Angola, the major commercial bank.   Together,
    the two account for 87 percent of financial operations.
    The issuing bank is now called Banco Nacional de Ango-
    la, while the major commercial bank was renamed Banco
    Popular de Angola.

BEATRICE OF KONGO (DONA BEATRIX).   c. 1682(?)-1706.
    A young aristocratic Kongo woman, Beatrice claimed to
    have died and to have been resurrected as Saint Anthony
    of Padua.   She preached a syncretic Christianity, attack-
    ing Catholic missionaries and Roman rituals and doc-
    trines, claiming that Christ was born and baptized in
    Kongo, and that the Madonna was black.   She performed
    miracles, raised messianic hopes, and attracted a sub-
    stantial number of followers.   The rise and fall of Bea-
    trice must be seen in the context of traditional Kongo
    religion and in the contemporary political situation.
    Civil strife with several lineages claiming the office of
    manikongo was endemic in the latter part of the seven-
    teenth century.   Beatrice was seen as a religious liabil-
    ity by Capuchin missionaries and as a political threat by
    African opponents, since she supported the claims of the
    Kimpanzu clan.   When the rival Kimulaza clan triumphed
    and Pedro IV became manikongo, she was arrested in
    1706 and burned at the stake.   See ANTONIAN MOVE-
    MENT.

BENGUELA, town and province.   Benguela was established
    by the Portuguese in 1617 as part of a southern expan-
    sion from Luanda in search of new ports and sources of
    trade.   Access to the interior was difficult because of
    the high peaks of the Benguela Highlands, and the mili-
    tary post of Caconda on the plateau edge was only estab-
    lished in 1682.   In the eighteenth and nineteenth cen-
    turies Ovimbundu traders and Portuguese agents, pom-
    beiros and sertanejos, opened up an active trade across
    the Central Highlands, and Benguela became a major en-
    trepôt in the slave trade, dispatching ships directly, or
    via Luanda, to Brazil.   At times Benguela was quite
    isolated from the capital.   It had its own Governor, a
    subordinate of the Governor-General in Luanda.
        In 1970 Benguela was the fourth-largest city of
    Angola and with Lobito, 20 miles to the north, part of

the most important urban complex in the country outside
of Luanda.   In its own right, Benguela is a historic trading and fishing center and the administrative center of
the province.

BENGUELA RAILWAY (Companhia do Caminho de Ferro de
Benguela).   Starting from Lobito on the Atlantic Coast
the Benguela Railway crosses Angola to reach the Zaire
frontier near Dilolo on the Zaire border, a distance of
838 miles.   Here it connects with the Zaire rail system,
which continues into the mineral-rich Shaba province and
south into the Zambian copperbelt.   The sole rail link to
the Atlantic, the Benguela Railway has been an essential
outlet for the Zaire and Zambian copper industries.   In
Angola the railway serves the agricultural and commercial centers of the central plateau and the diamond industry, the railhead of which is Luena (Luso).   A victim
of the dislocation caused by civil strife in Angola since
independence, the Benguela Railway has operated only in
limited sections, 1975-78.   It was officially reopened in
an agreement between Zaire and Angola in November
1978.
        Construction of the railway began in 1903 as an
Anglo-Portuguese enterprise financed by the British-con-
trolled Tanganyika Concessions Limited.   The line reached
the Katanga province of Belgium Congo in 1929.

BIE (BIHE), Ovimbundu state.   With Bailundu, Bié had
emerged as the dominant Ovimbundu state by the eighteenth century.   Bié's prosperity was based on its pre-
eminence in the long-distance trade from Benguela to the
Upper Zambezi.   The commercial and strategic importance of the area attracted sertanejos, and, by the end of
the nineteenth century, Portuguese and Boer farmers and
traders.   Portuguese forces defeated Ndunduma, the soba
of Bié, in 1890, and he was captured and deported.
Some Bié forces may have participated in the Bailundu
revolt, 1902-04, but the main resistance to Portuguese
advance was over.   See OVIMBUNDU.

BIE, town and province.   Previously called Silva Porto after
the famous sertanejo of that name, this was an important
center for Ovimbundu and Portuguese traders on the route
from Benguela to the interior by the mid-nineteenth century.   Situated on the eastern side of the Central Highlands and on the Benguela railway, Bié is the administrative capital of the province and an agricultural and commercial center.

BOAVIDA, AMERICO (Ngola Kimbanda). 20 November 1923-
25 September 1968. Doctor and nationalist leader.
Born in Luanda, Boavida was one of the first Angolans
to graduate from the Liceu Salvador Correa in Luanda.
He studied medicine in the universities of Porto and Lisbon and in 1952 graduated as a doctor. He also did
clinical work at the University of Barcelona, and post-
graduate studies at the University of Prague. From
1955 to 1960 he practiced medicine in Luanda. Boavida
joined MPLA in 1960 and became director of the newly
established medical service for refugees in Léopoldville.
He was one of the first Angolan doctors to go to the
military front inside the country. In 1968 he was killed
during a Portuguese helicopter attack on an MPLA camp
in Moxico, where he was training medical technicians to
work with guerrillas.
     Boavida's critique of Portuguese colonialism, which
emphasized the economic determinants in Angolan history, has been translated into English as **Five Centuries
of Portuguese Exploitation.**

BOERS. Boer trekkers, refugees from British expansion in
South Africa, arrived in Angola in several migrations in
the period 1879-1905. By 1905 there were about 1, 500
Afrikaners in Angola, mainly living in the hinterland of
Mossamedes and Benguela. They introduced their ox-
wagons into the area and revolutionized the transport industry until they themselves were ruined by railways and
motorized vehicles. They also proved useful to the
Portuguese as mercenaries in suppressing African rebellions. The Boers were too independent, however. They
were not successful as sedentary farmers and rebuffed
attempts at cultural assimilation by the Portuguese. Relations soured, and in 1928 about 2, 000 Boers trekked
out of Angola to settle in Namibia, leaving only a few
remnants of their community behind.

-C-

CABINDA, port and province. The port of Cabinda, situated
about 30 miles north of the Zaire River, was a major
entrepôt in the slave trade of West Central Africa in the
eighteenth and nineteenth centuries. It attracted the attention of the Portuguese since it syphoned off slaves
that might otherwise have reached the Luanda market.
An attempt to build a fort there in 1783 was short-lived,

it being destroyed by the French the following year. In
1885 Cabinda came under Portuguese rule, and from
1887 to 1917 it was the capital of Congo district. Although a good anchorage, Cabinda's port facilities are
little developed. A main source of business in the twentieth century has been Cabinda's status as a free port.
    The enclave of Cabinda is separated from Angola
by a strip of Zaire territory but has been administered
as an integral part of Angola since 1885. The status of
the enclave is contested by the secessionist group FLEC,
which demands independence. The position of the enclave
and its relation to Angola is crucial because of its oil
resources; timber, cocoa, coffee, phosphates, and potas-
sium also contribute to the wealth of the region. See
FLEC; OIL.

CACIMBO.   The cacimbo season is the dry season from May
    to September. The name derives from the heavy morning
    mist during this time of the year.

CAMBAMBE.   The Cambambe Falls mark the limit of navi-
    gation on the Kwanza River. Supposed silver mines en-
    couraged the Portuguese to advance inland through
    Mbundu territory to this point, which they reached in
    1604, only to find the mines were nonexistent. They
    proceeded to build a fort (presídio) at Cambambe.
        The first phase of the Cambambe dam near Dondo
    was completed in 1963. It provides more than enough
    hydroelectric power for the Luanda area.

CÃO, DIOGO. d. 1486? Portuguese navigator and leader of
    the first European expedition to reach the mouth of the
    Zaire River, in 1483. He established contact with the
    inhabitants of the Kongo kingdom--the first between Afri-
    cans and Europeans in Angolan history--and explored
    further south to a point beyond Benguela before turning
    back. He made a second voyage to Kongo in 1485-86,
    visiting the capital of the manikongo and sailing south
    along the coast as far as the area of modern Namibia,
    where he probably died.

CAPITÃO-MOR (pl. CAPITÃES-MORES; lit. captain-major).
    A military officer appointed to rule over an area in the
    hinterland of the colony, sometimes based at a small
    fort and commanding a few troops.

CARREIRA, HENRIQUE TELES (IKO). Born 6 February
    1933, a mestiço from Luanda and a cousin of Mário de

Andrade, Carreira came to prominence in MPLA in
1962, when he was elected the movement's executive in
charge of security at its First National Conference in
Léopoldville.   He became an officer in the guerrilla army taking responsibility for Cabinda operations and later
became a commander on the eastern front.   In 1970 he
was appointed to MPLA's five-member Political and
Military Coordinating Committee.

In September 1974 Carreira became a member of
MPLA's Political Bureau and Central Committee.   He
helped negotiate Cuban aid to MPLA forces in 1975 and
was appointed Minister of Defense in Neto's government.

CHIPENDA, DANIEL JULIO.   May 1931- .   An Ovimbundu
from Central Angola, Chipenda's father, Rev. Jesse
Chipenda, was the first General-Secretary of the Church
Council of Central Angola.   He was arrested in 1968 and
died in prison the following year.

Daniel Chipenda was an important early member
of MPLA, the leading Ovimbundu, who had a considerable
personal fellowing in the Lobito-Benguela area.   In 1964
he headed MPLA's Youth Wing and in the late 1960s was
a member of the movement's Steering Committee responsible for Information and Publicity.   In 1970 he was appointed to the five-member Political and Military Coordinating Committee.   He became a top commander in the
guerrilla forces on the eastern front.

In 1973 Chipenda split with Neto in the "Eastern
Revolt, " taking with him a personal following of some
2, 000 troops and seriously weakening MPLA's ranks.   In
October 1974 he was expelled from the party and in 1975
formed a loose alliance with Roberto, who made him
Secretary-General of FNLA.   Chipenda's Ovimbundu following and the troops he brought with him were an important addition to FNLA's ranks.   Chipenda's forces
fought the South Africans on the southern front in the
1975-76 war, but his army disintegrated following defeats
by MPLA and Cuban forces in January 1976.   Chipenda
is said to have fled to Zaire or Namibia.

CHOKWE (COKWE, TSCHOKWE, QUIOCO).   Lunda emigrants
settled among the Chokwe of eastern Angola some time
before the seventeenth century.   They established small
chiefdoms and forged political and cultural ties.   The
Chokwe remained an insignificant and little-known people,
however, until the mid-nineteenth century, when they exploited their skills as hunters and gatherers to enter the

west coast ivory, wax, and rubber trade and at the same
time began a rapid expansion using the guns and wealth
they acquired in the trade.   Through intermarriage and
conquest Chokwe influence and culture spread to neighboring peoples--Lunda, Luena, Luchazi, and others.   In
1885 Chokwe raiders sacked the Lunda capital, and by
the end of the nineteenth century they occupied a territory about four times the size of their original homeland.
Today Chokwe and "Chokwe-ized" groups are scattered
through Lunda, Moxico, Bié, and Cuando-Cubango districts and number about half a million.   See LUNDA.

COFFEE.   Coffee production began in Angola in the 1830s
and 1840s, and it quickly became an important cash
crop.   Until it was overtaken by oil in 1973, coffee was
the leading export through much of the twentieth century.
In 1974 Angola was the second producer in Africa (after
Ivory Coast) and the fourth in the world.   Most of the
coffee crop belongs to the robusta species, a particularly
important base in many blends because of its relative
cheapness compared to the top grade arabica.   The main
coffee-growing regions are Uige, Zaire, North and South
Kwanza, and, to a lesser extent, Cabinda.

Output has fallen sharply as a result of the wars
of independence; the 1976 estimate was about one-third
of the prewar level.   Major problems have been labor
shortages and a lack of trained management.   In particular, the Ovimbundu who were contracted by the Portuguese in the colonial period to work on the northern
plantations have been reluctant to move out of their own
region.   MPLA has recruited volunteer brigades to help
with the coffee harvest, but these lack experience and
are not enough.   The Angola Coffee Institute is training
technicians to manage the industry in place of the expatriates who left.   Production is now organized through
co-ops of small farmers; large state-owned plantations
that have taken over those abandoned; and privately run
coffee farms owned by those who remained after independence.

COLONATOS.   Planned rural settlements sponsored by the
colonial government as a means of expanding the Portuguese presence in the interior.   See SETTLERS.

COLONOS.   White agricultural settlers.   In the case of Angola the settlers were usually poor, lacking in capital,
and with little previous knowledge of farming.   Many

quickly gave up and turned to commerce.   See SET-
TLERS.

CONFERÊNCIA DAS ORGANIZAÇÕES NACIONALISTAS DAS
COLONIAS PORTUGUESAS.   The Conference of Nationalist Organizations of the Portuguese Colonies was formed
in Casablanca in April 1961.   It was an attempt to for-
malize and increase the links between the four socialist
parties of the Portuguese African colonies, that is,
MPLA (Angola), FRELIMO (Mozambique), PAIGC (Guinea-
Bissau and Cape Verde Islands), and MLSTP (São Tomé
and Príncipe).   The main activities were joint lobbying
and propaganda work, especially at the OAU, and the
exchange of military information.   The chief external
support came from the USSR and other socialist countries.

CONTRATADOS.   A general term for African contract laborers, many of whom were in fact forced into service
and never entered into a written contract.   First established in decrees of 1875 and 1899, just as slavery was
abolished, the system had the effect of legalizing the
continued exploitation of African workers.   It was not
until 1962 that, following the revolts of the previous year
and international pressure through the International Labor
Organization, forced labor by Africans was made illegal.

CORDEIRO DA MATTA, JOAQUIM DIAS.   1857-94.   Writer,
folklorist, historian, linguist.   Born in Cabiri, Luanda
district, Cordeiro da Matta was an outstanding African
intellectual and nationalist who sought to reestablish the
values of traditional Angolan culture.   His concerns
were reflected in his many writings, for example a collection of over 700 Kimbundu proverbs and riddles
(1891), a Kimbundu grammar (1892), and a Kimbundu-
Portuguese dictionary (1893).   He also wrote several
historical essays, short stories, and poetry.

COTONANG (Companhia Geral dos Algodões de Angola).
The largest of several cotton-growing companies, Cotonang had a concession in the Cassanje region east of
Malanje.   The local people were forced to cultivate cotton and to sell their crops at low prices fixed by the
government.   In January 1961 the workers went on strike
and refused to pay taxes as a protest against the abuses
of the system.   Reprisals by the Portuguese resulted
in villages being destroyed and Africans killed.   This

"cotton revolt" was a precursor of the nationalist uprisings of February-March 1961.

Cotonang was nationalized in 1978 along with several other foreign firms abandoned by their owners.

COUP ATTEMPT.   On 27 May 1977 there was an unsuccessful attempt to overthrow the Neto government through a coup d'état.   Several MPLA leaders were killed, including Saydi Mingus, the Minister of Finance.   The coup attempt may be attributed to several factors: for example, popular discontent with the government generated by the dislocation that followed the civil war and the departure of most Portuguese--this included problems of food production and distribution and the failure of essential services; ideological dissension within MPLA--this was apparent at several levels, including the inhabitants of the musseques in Luanda, who had been encouraged by notions of "people's power" to set up their own committees; discontent coalescing around the person of Nito Alves, a grass-roots African leader with considerable charisma who stood apart from and provided a popular alternative to the mestiço intellectuals who dominated the MPLA government.

CRUZ, VIRIATO FRANCISCO CLEMENTE DA.   Poet and nationalist leader.   Born in 1928 in Porto Amboim, S. Kwanza district, Viriato da Cruz received his secondary education in Luanda.   He was an initiator of a nationalist, intellectual movement in Angola in the 1940s and 1950s and was editor of the radical literary magazine Mensagem.   He published many poems and articles in journals, and also a volume of poems (1961).

His nationalist activities forced da Cruz to flee from PIDE to Europe in 1957.   He was a founding member of MPLA and its first General-Secretary, 1956-62. His extreme left-wing views and his concern for international socialism brought him into conflict with others in MPLA, including Neto.   In 1963 he and a group of supporters broke away from the movement.   Da Cruz's attempts to conclude a lasting alliance with Holden Roberto failed, the latter being suspicious of da Cruz's ideology and pro-Chinese stance.   From 1969 to 1973 he lived in Peking, where he was Secretary of the Organization of Asian and African writers.   He died in relative obscurity in 1973.

CUANDO-CUBANGO, province.   Situated in the southeastern corner of Angola on the borders of Zambia and Namibia,

Cuando-Cubango province is one of the most remote and least densely populated areas of Angola. The major river, the Cubango, enters the Okavango Swamp in Botswana, and its tributaries are seasonal. East of the Cubango the area is better watered, with permanent rivers, tall grass, and scattered forests. There is cattle-raising and potential for timber production. The broad and even-flowing Cuando River, a tributary of the Zambezi, is a useful waterway for the people of the area. The capital, Menongue (Serpa Pinto), is linked to the Atlantic Coast by the Mossamedes Railway.

CUBANS. The arrival of Cuban troops in Angola in October-November 1975 tipped the balance in the civil war in favor of MPLA. By March 1976 the threat from the opposing forces of FNLA, UNITA, and their allies had largely been eliminated. Since 1976 Cuba has provided social and economic assistance as well as military aid. Cuban experts have been important in replacing expatriates who left at independence. They have aided the RPA in diverse fields, such as public health, education, construction, engineering, fishing, communications, and agricultural production.

CUNENE RIVER. The Cunene River rises in the Bié plateau not far from Huambo and flows southward across the Huíla Plateau until at the Ruacana Falls it turns sharply westward and forms 200 miles of border between Angola and Namibia before reaching the Atlantic. Only some 600 miles long, the river has important hydroelectric potential, since its bed drops one mile from source to mouth. It is also important for irrigation, especially in the central and southwestern sections of its course, where many of the tributaries are empty in the dry season.

CUNENE RIVER HYDROELECTRIC PROJECT. An agreement to harness the waters of the Cunene River for power and irrigation was first concluded between South Africa and Portugal in 1926, at the time when the border between Namibia and Angola was delineated. The total project, which includes twenty-seven dams and power stations, is designed to increase the area under irrigation in southwestern Angola twenty-five to thirty times, and a vast transmission grid is to carry power to South Africa, Namibia, and Angola. In 1969 the first phase of development was agreed on, giving Portugal control over the in-

stallations from the source to Calueque, and South Africa
from Calueque to the mouth. South Africa was responsible for the bulk of the finance. It was projected that by
1978 work on five main dams, at Gove, Matala, Matun-
to, Calueque, and Ruacana Falls, would be completed.
In 1976 the MPLA government suspended work at the
important Calueque dam. Although South Africa finished
three of the five generators at Ruacana Falls in 1978,
power could not flow to Namibia, since the Angolan government, which controls the river upstream, refused to
divert the water. It argues that it does not deal with
South Africa and will only negotiate with a legitimate,
free, independent Namibian government, which from
MPLA's point of view is that of SWAPO.
        Thus, the Cunene River scheme is a major poli-
tical issue in the area. Major criticisms have also been
leveled on economic and social grounds. It is argued
that the major beneficiaries in Namibia will be the mining companies and white urban areas; and that the im-
proved water supply will aid the development of the Ovambo Bantustan. It is also argued that in Angola the
scheme was conceived to serve white farming and industrial interests and that the impact on local African economies will be disastrous. The traditional ecological
balance will be upset; land used by Africans for grazing
will be flooded; and if local populations, previously transhumant pastoralists, are resettled as sedentary farmers,
enormous problems will be created.

CURRENCY. In January 1977 Angola broke its link with the
    Portuguese currency area and issued its own currency,
    the Kwanza (1 Kwanza = 100 lwei). The Kwanza has
    been declared nonconvertible in the international market
    by the Angolan government and is not quoted on interna-
    tional exchanges.

                        -D-

DEGREDADOS. Prisoners who were exiled from Portugal to
    Angola to serve out their sentence. They were the basis
    of the colony's settler population before the twentieth
    century. See SETTLERS.

DEMBOS. Wooded hill country about 100 miles northeast of
    Luanda and between the Bengo and Loge Rivers. The
    term Dembos is also used for the inhabitants of the re-

gion. Living in the Kongo-Mbundu borderlands, the
Dembos (Ndembu) are usually included in the broad Kim-
bundu-speaking group, although they are strongly influenced by the Kikongo-speakers to the north as well.
In spite of the proximity of the area to Luanda,
the Dembos have a long history of resistance to Portuguese penetration, for example, in armed resistance to
colonial forces 1907-09 and 1917-19. After the outbreak
of the Wars of Liberation in 1961 the Dembos became a
center of guerrilla resistance and was organized as
MPLA's First Military Region.

DEMOCRATIC PEOPLE'S REPUBLIC OF ANGOLA. Established in November 1975, with a coalition government of
FNLA and UNITA in Huambo, and a northern "capital"
at Ambriz. This was an attempted response to MPLA's
establishment of the RPA. The DPRA never managed to
organize, since FNLA and UNITA could seldom cooper-
ate, and it was never recognized, the final blow being
the OAU's recognition of Neto's government in February
1976.

DIAMANG (Companhia de Diamantes de Angola). Established
in 1917, the formal concession of the Angola Diamond
Company covered almost the whole of Angola until 1971,
when other consortia were granted concessions. Diamang, an amalgam of Belgian, British, American, and
South African interests, largely confined its activities
to the northeastern corner of Lunda district. From its
center of operations at Dundo the company virtually assumed sovereignty over the region, controlling employ-
ment, schools, and medical services and operating a
security force.
Diamonds have been a top export earner in the
twentieth century. Production fell by about two-thirds,
1975-76, following the departure of skilled personnel.
In 1977 a majority of the Company's shares were nationalized.
In 1947 the Company founded a museum at Dundo
particularly concerned with Lunda-Chokwe ethnography; it
published a useful collection of monographs.

DIAS DE NOVAIS, PAULO. d. 1589. The grandson of
Bartolemeu Dias, Paulo Dias was first sent to Angola
in 1559 on a diplomatic mission from the king of Portugal to the Ndongo ruler. Paulo Dias arrived at the
Ndongo court along with four missionaries in 1561 but

was kept a prisoner there for four years. On returning
to Portugal, he was instrumental in helping to form the
new policy, which involved the establishment of a colony
through military conquest in Angola. He was appointed
donatário in 1571.
        His expedition arrived at Luanda Island in 1575
and established a settlement on the mainland opposite in
1576. From there he launched an offensive along the
Kwanza into Mbundu territory in 1579. At the time of
his death ten years later he had advanced only about 70
miles into the interior in the face of Mbundu resistance.

DONATARIO. During the sixteenth century the Portuguese
    colonies were given to nobles, who became the propri-
    etors (donatários), with administrative and fiscal author-
    ity over the area as well as certain responsibilities.
    Paulo Dias de Novais was appointed the first donatário
    of Angola in 1571.

-E-

"EASTERN REVOLT" (Revolta do Leste). A breakaway by
    Daniel Chipenda and about 2,000 troops loyal to him
    from the ranks of MPLA, 1973-74. These constituted
    an important part of the guerrilla forces on the eastern
    front and seriously weakened MPLA's position. See
    CHIPENDA.

ECONOMY. Agriculture is the basis of Angola's economy,
    involving about 80 percent of the labor force. The basic
    food crops are maize, manioc, beans, millet, and sor-
    ghum. The major cash crops are coffee, cotton, sisal,
    sugar, and maize. Rearing livestock is a little-developed
    but potentially important activity of southern Angola.
    Fish products have also been a significant export item.
    Mineral reserves include oil, diamonds, and iron.
    These together with coffee were the cornerstones of the
    economy in the latter part of the colonial period.
        After 1961 Portugal reversed its long-standing
    policy of severely restricting the investment of foreign
    capital in its colonies, and American, West European,
    and South African capital flowed into Angola, resulting in
    expansion of agriculture, heavy industry, manufacturing,
    hydroelectric plants, communication networks, and con-
    struction projects. Many key economic activities ground
    to a halt as a result of the civil war at independence, the

check on foreign capital, and the exodus of European
management and technicians. Of the major industries,
only oil production remained close to its prewar level.
The MPLA government is dedicated to the creation of a socialist economy, with the state playing the
leading role in planning and production. A 1976 Law of
State Intervention outlined the three sectors of the
planned economy: 1) state organizations and the gradual
nationalization of "strategic" industries; 2) cooperatives;
3) private enterprises, which will continue but be re-
duced in number. In 1976 a National Planning Council
was established to oversee the development of the economy based on socialist objectives. A Three-Year Development Plan was launched in 1977; and a Five-Year
Plan will start in 1980. See COFFEE; DIAMANG;
IRON; OIL.

EDUCATION. At the time of independence the literacy rate
was in the region of 10-15 percent. The MPLA government has promoted an education policy with four predominant themes: 1) free, universal education; 2) nationalization of education--there will be no private
schools; the mission schools, which were largely responsible for primary education in the colonial period, will
eventually have to relinquish control; 3) education should
be linked to production; thus, a basic aim will be to
satisfy the manpower needs of the country; 4) education
will be based on ideas of "people's power"; thus, there
will be constant consultation between teachers, students,
and workers.
        The lack of trained personnel, especially following
the departure of most Portuguese teachers, means that
this education policy can only be implemented very slow-
ly. See MISSIONARIES; ASSIMILADO.

EXERCITO DE LIBERTAÇÃO NACIONAL DE ANGOLA. The
guerrilla army of FNLA. ELNA's main military base
was across the frontier at Kinkuzu in Zaire; its main
field of operations was the Kongo and Dembos regions of
northern Angola, although after 1968 it also opened an
eastern front from a camp near Kolwezi in southwestern
Zaire.

EXERCITO POPULAR DE LIBERTAÇÃO DE ANGOLA.
MPLA's guerrilla army, which became FAPLA in August
1974. During the Wars of Liberation, 1961-74, EPLA
opened up several military fronts: the First Political-

Military Region in the Dembos and Nambuangongo; the
Second in Cabinda; the Third in Moxico and Cuando-
Cubango; the Fourth in Lunda and Malanje; the Fifth in
Bié; the Sixth in Cunene. See FAPLA.

-F-

FALCÃO, EUSEBIO DE LEMOS PINHEIRO. 1818-51. A Lu-
anda-born mestiço, he was one of the most distinguished
Angolan lawyers of the nineteenth century. He was educated at Coimbra University in Portugal and served as a
commissioner on the Court of Mixed Commission and
Arbitration, established in the 1840s to adjudicate cases
deriving from the abolition of the slave trade.

FEIRA. A market or fair. Especially used in Portuguese
literature for points in the interior where their agents
did business with African traders.

FONTES PEREIRA, JOSE DE. 1823-91. Journalist, lawyer, and nationalist. A mestiço born in Luanda or its
environs, Fontes Pereira was at first a loyal assimilado
who worked for the Portuguese as a civil servant. He
entered politics late, publishing his first article in the
radical journal O Cruzeiro do Sul in 1873. Quickly gain-
ing a reputation as a scourge of the colonial administration, he published articles in eight Luanda weekly papers
and four Lisbon journals. His articles attacked various
aspects of Portuguese rule, for example, the use of
forced labor, the shipment of African workers to São
Tomé, the need for more schools, prison conditions,
and discrimination at all levels against non-Portuguese.
At the same time, although a republican, Fontes Pereira
remained loyal to Portugal, even advocating further
Portuguese expansion in the Angolan interior.
    Between 1883 and 1890 a marked change took
place in his writings, as he showed total disillusionment
with Portugal and lost all hope of improvement of conditions for Angolans. He moved away from mainstream
assimilado protest and advocated full Angolan independence. In 1890 he even suggested Britain should take
over Portuguese possessions in Africa.
    Long socially ostracized, Fontes Pereira was de-
nounced as a traitor by the Governor-General and dismissed from his job. He died in disgrace a short time
after in 1891.

FORÇAS ARMADAS POPULAR PARA LIBERTAÇÃO DE
ANGOLA. FAPLA was formed from the existing MPLA
guerrilla forces in August 1974. In November 1975 it
was institutionalized as the national army under Article
6 of the constitution of the PRA. In October 1976 a
Five-Year Plan for Organization and Equipment to trans-
form FAPLA into a modern army was initiated. This
will be done with aid from Cuba, the Soviet Union, and
Eastern European countries. See ARMED FORCES;
EPLA.

FORCED LABOR. The exploitation of African labor was a
constant theme in Angolan history from the fifteenth century until independence. The slave trade was officially
abolished in 1836 and slavery in 1878, but the sparse
and scattered population of Angola and the shortage of
labor meant that Portuguese colonial administrations accepted forced labor as a means of providing the work
force necessary for economic development. Compulsory
labor was made illegal in 1962, but abuses continued until the end of the colonial period. See CONTRATADOS;
SERVIÇAES; SLAVE TRADE.

FRENTE DEMOCRATICA DE LIBERTAÇÃO DE ANGOLA.
An alliance formed in July 1963 by MPLA, UNTA
(MPLA's Trade Union organization), and three small
Kongo ethnonationalist parties, the MNA, MDIA, and
Ngwizako. This was negotiated by Neto at a time of
MPLA weakness and FNLA strength. But the plan back-
fired, since it was seen as an unacceptable compromise
by several MPLA factions, including groups led by Viri-
ato da Cruz and Mário de Andrade. By 1965 the FDLA
had disintegrated.

FRENTE NACIONAL DE LIBERTAÇÃO DE ANGOLA (FNLA).
Formed at the end of March 1962 by an alliance of the
UPA and PDA, FNLA was always dominated by the UPA
group led by Holden Roberto, who often assumed dictatorial powers. Although it attracted a multiethnic leadership, FNLA largely remained an ethnonationalist party
depending on its traditional Kongo mass following. On
5 April 1962 FNLA created GRAE to assume overall responsibility for the political and military struggle against
the Portuguese.
        FNLA guerrillas were most active in northern
Angola, operating from bases in Zaire, with the military
headquarters at Kinkuzu. In the 1960s FNLA received

covert aid from the United States through the CIA in
Zaire. In 1972-73 FNLA received military aid from
China through the mediation of Nyerere of Tanzania.
In October 1974 FNLA opened an office in Luanda
and began to organize its support in the capital. Roberto
bought the newspaper A Província de Angola and a TV
station to disseminate propaganda. FNLA's participation
in the Transitional Government that was to lead Angola
to independence broke down when MPLA troops ousted
FNLA forces from Luanda in July 1975. Then the FNLA
army, enlarged by Chipenda's troops and supported by
Portuguese and South African forces, won major battles
in the escalating civil war and by November 1975 had
advanced to within a few miles from Luanda only to be
turned back by FAPLA with Cuban reinforcements.
In November 1975 FNLA with UNITA established
a rival government to that of MPLA, but this was never
recognized, and by January 1976 FNLA opposition had
collapsed. Most leaders retreated to exile in Zaire, and
FNLA maintained a low-level military activity in the
Kongo regions of northern Angola from Zaire bases.
See EPLA; GRAE; PDA; ROBERTO; UPA.

FRENTE PARA A LIBERTAÇÃO DO ENCLAVE DE CABIN-
DA. Formed in 1963 by several Cabindan nationalist
groups at a conference in Pointe-Noire, the Front for
the Liberation of the Enclave of Cabinda aims to achieve
Cabindan independence from the rest of Angola. Since
November 1974, when it was banned in the enclave,
FLEC has organized itself militarily, launching several
attacks from Zaire on MPLA and Cuban forces, but with
little success. The Cabindan independence movement
has suffered through its history from personal rivalries
and internal division that have hopelessly weakened its
efforts. The wealth of the Cabindan oil fields has been
an important factor in drawing external support to FLEC,
notably from Zaire, Gabon, and France.

-G-

GOVERNO REVOLUCIONARIO DE ANGOLA NO EXILIO. The
Revolutionary Government of Angola in Exile was formed
on 5 April 1962. Technically, it was an alliance of
Roberto's UPA, Kunzika's PDA, and the da Cruz faction
of MPLA. In practice, it was dominated by Roberto's
group. GRAE was based in Kinshasa, where it estab-

lished related organizations, for example, SARA, which
worked among the quarter-million Kongo refugees in
Zaire; AMA, the women's organization; UNEA, students'
group; JFNLA, youth wing; LGTA, trade-union movement.
      Holden Roberto's greatest political victory over
Neto's MPLA came in 1963, when the OAU recognized
GRAE as the only viable representative of the Angolan
liberation movement and voted to channel all military aid
to GRAE alone. Another success for Roberto was the
victory of Mobutu, a personal friend, in the political
struggle in Zaire. GRAE, on the other hand, was
weakened by the defection of its Foreign Minister, Savimbi, and his Ovimbundu supporters, who broke away
to form their own party, UNITA.
      By 1971 dissatisfaction with Roberto's leadership,
the weakness of GRAE, and rising support for Neto
caused the OAU to withdraw formal recognition. GRAE
gradually faded away, although the FNLA continued.
See FNLA; PDA; ROBERTO.

GRÊMIO AFRICANO. Formed by a moderate group of Luanda-based assimilados in 1913, the Grêmio Africano was
a breakaway group from the Liga Angolana. Its moderate aims chiefly concerned the improvement of the educational and social conditions of mestiços and Africans.
In 1921 the Grêmio Africano was allowed by Norton de
Matos to choose representatives to serve on the Legislative Council, but by 1923 it had virtually been silenced,
when the Governor-General reversed his policy and
moved to suppress emerging Angolan nationalism. In
1929-30 the group was allowed to reform as ANANGOLA,
a government-sponsored cultural-social organization.

GUERRA PRETA (lit. "black war"). The "second-line" colonial army, consisting of African troops. See ARMED
FORCES.

                          -H-

HERERO. The 20,000 Herero of southwestern Angola live
mainly in the hot, arid coastal lowlands and in the
mountainous escarpment to the east, in Mossamedes,
Benguela, and Huíla provinces. Traditionally nomadic
or seminomadic pastoralists, they were not much noted
by the Portuguese, since they lived in a harsh and little-

sought-after environment. Disputes with African neighbors and white settlers over cattle, as well as refusal
to adapt to colonial society and pay taxes, finally caused
the Portuguese to launch a military expedition against
the Cuvale, a main Herero subgroup, in 1940-41. Hundreds were killed and imprisoned, hundreds more were
sent to labor in mines and plantations in Angola and
São Tomé, whilst others migrated south to join the main
Herero group in Namibia.

HUAMBO, town, province. A Portuguese corruption of the
name of the Ovimbundu state in the Central Highlands,
Wambu. Situated on a fertile plateau about 250 miles
from the coast, at an altitude of nearly 5, 800 feet and
in one of the most favorable climatic regions in Angola,
Huambo (Nova Lisboa) is a principal Ovimbundu center
and has been a magnet for white settlers in the twentieth
century. It is a major commercial, agricultural, and
administrative center and contains the main workshops
for the Benguela Railway. In 1970 Nova Lisboa was the
second-largest city in Angola after Luanda. It was the
focal point for UNITA activities, 1974-76.

HUILA, province. The Huíla Highlands cover an area of approximately 2, 500 square miles. The highest peaks in
the Humpata Highlands in the west reach 6, 000-7, 500
feet, while to the east the land slopes gently to the vast,
flat Huíla plateau. This is the traditional homeland of
the Nyaneka peoples, Huíla being the name of one of several small Nyaneka states that existed in the mid-nineteenth century.
     Pombeiros from Luanda and Benguela, and Ovim-
bundu from Huambo, traded in ivory, wax, slaves, and
cattle in the region by the eighteenth century. By the
early nineteenth century the Portuguese had appointed a
regente for the area, and in 1845 the settlement at Huíla
became the site of a presídio. Like the Huambo and
Bié area to the north, the cool climate and farming potential of the western and northern regions of the plateau
attracted white settlers--Madeirans, Brazilians, Portuguese, and Boers--in the nineteenth century. By the
early twentieth century Sá da Bandeira (Lubango) was becoming the most important urban center in southern Angola. Communications with the coast were facilitated
by the completion of the railway from Mossamedes to Sá
da Bandeira in 1923. See LUBANGO; MOSSAMEDES;
NYANEKA.

-I-

IMBANGALA. The term Imbangala is derived from an Umbundu root, vangala, meaning to be brave or to wander
widely through the countryside. In the sixteenth century
Lunda title-holders and their followers, who had gradually moved westward from their homeland east of the
Kwango, arrived in Ovimbundu territory, fused Ovimbundu political and social ideas with their own, and began a new period in their history, becoming known as
the Imbangala. They formed militarized and highly mobile bands that roved freely through the region of Benguela and north to the Kwanza, pillaging and terrorizing
the societies they encountered. The Imbangala were
ideal allies for the Portuguese, who wanted to intensify
their conquest of Mbundu areas and expand the slave
trade. An Imbangala-Portuguese agreement was concluded in 1612, and for the next decade their joint forces
attacked the sedentary Mbundu, bringing the state of
Ndongo and its neighbors to the point of total collapse.
By the mid-seventeenth century the Imbangala had settled
down among the Mbundu to form a new group of states,
which existed until the nineteenth century. See KA-
SANJE; MATAMBA; MBUNDU.

INDIGENA (lit., a native). Under the policy of the "New
State, " the indígenas were treated as a separate legal
category in the population with none of the rights of
Portuguese citizens. The only way an African could
escape from this status was through education and quali-
fying as an assimilado. Classified as indígenas, the
mass of the population thus had no rights while being
subject to oppressive taxation and forced labor. The
status was legally abolished after the rebellions of 1961,
of which the discrimination inherent in the indígena policy
was a prime cause. See ASSIMILADO.

IRON. Iron-working technology has been crucial in the political, economic, and social development of Bantu societies in Angola since at least the first millennium A.D.
The modern extractive industry dates from the 1950s,
when a high level of active prospecting led to the exploitation of deposits in the districts of Luanda, North
Kwanza, Huambo, Bié, and Huíla. The most important
sources were at Cassinga in Huíla district, where the
highest grade ore, with 68-percent iron content, was discovered. First exploited by the Portuguese-controlled

Companhia Mineira do Lobito, the largest investments
were made 1965-75 by the Krupp Company of West Germany, which developed the mines and built a rail link to
the Mossamedes railway. In this period iron, together
with coffee, oil, and diamonds, was one of Angola's top
exports. Production at Cassinga halted in 1975 and had
not resumed in 1977. The high-grade ore has already
been extracted, and massive investments are needed for
further development.

IVORY. Although an established item of trade from the ear-
liest period of Portuguese contact with Angola, it was
only after the abolition of the slave trade in 1836 that
demand for ivory at Luanda, Benguela, and Mossamedes
soared, and elephant-hunting and ivory-trading in the interior became a source of great prosperity. The abolition of the royal monopoly on ivory exports also stimulated the trade after 1834.
    The trade through the Kongo areas of northern
Angola to the markets at Malebo Pool (around the area
of present-day Kinshasa) had been established since the
sixteenth century. In the nineteenth century Chokwe
hunters and Ovimbundu traders searched out sources of
ivory east of the Kwango, and the Ovambo and Nkhumbi
of southern Angola sold ivory to Portuguese and Boer
traders.

-J-

JACINTO (DE AMARAL MARTINS), ANTONIO. Poet, writer,
nationalist. Born in 1932 in Luanda, Jacinto published
a volume of poems in 1961, and in the same year was
arrested on political charges by the colonial authorities.
He was condemned to fourteen years' imprisonment,
mostly spent in the prison of Tarrafal, Cape Verde Islands. Since independence Jacinto has had considerable
influence in forming the new educational policy. He was
appointed Minister of Education and Culture in Neto's
first Cabinet and in 1977 was Secretary of the National
Cultural Council.

JAGA. A term in general use in European literature of the
sixteenth and seventeenth centuries to denote peoples who
threatened the western coastal populations from the interior. Usually depicted as fierce, hostile, and mobile
forces, the "Jaga" were at one time thought to be a

single identifiable ethnic group. Recent research has underlined the application of the term to different peoples. Thus, the "Jaga" who invaded the Kongo kingdom in 1568, sacked the capital, and caused the ruler to flee to an island in the Zaire River were probably part of a local uprising against the ruling elite; whilst the "Jaga" who invaded the Mbundu-Ovimbundu areas in the sixteenth and seventeenth centuries have been identified as the Imbangala.

-K-

KASANJE. The highly centralized state founded by the Imbangala, after their retreat from the Portuguese, among the eastern Mbundu of the Baixa de Cassanje and the Kwango Valley. After 1648 Kasanje became the middleman on the major slave-trading route from Luanda via Malanje to the Kwango and thence to Lunda territory. The Portuguese established a feira at the Kasanje capital in the seventeenth century, through which the ruler, the kinguri, monopolized the supply of slaves to coastal markets. By the late eighteenth century, however, the kinguri, were losing control of the trade on which their prosperity and power depended, and the centralized system of government started to decline. See IMBANGALA; MBUNDU; SLAVE TRADE.

KHOISAN. A compound name for the Khoi and San peoples, who live mainly in Namibia and Botswana but who are also found in the northern part of the Kalahari desert that extends into southern Angola. The Khoisan represent some of the oldest inhabitants of southern Africa who have been pushed into marginal areas by the expanding Bantu. In the 1960 census the Khoisan of Angola numbered only about 7, 000.

KISAMA. Area south of the Kwanza and some 30 miles inland from the sea, famous for its high-quality rock salt, which was an important trade item for the local Mbundu and for peoples of the interior. The Portuguese made several attempts to gain control of the area, its salt mines, and the southern banks of the Kwanza, but were only finally successful in the twentieth century.

KONGO. Language, Kikongo; important subgroups include the Solongo, Mushikongo, Sosso, Zombo, Yaka, Vili, Woyo,

Kongo, Sundi, and Yombe. The Kongo of northern Angola are principally located in the provinces of Zaire,
Uige, and Cabinda. Numbering about 700, 000, they are
the third-largest ethnic group in Angola. They spill
over the frontiers of modern nation-states and are found
in large numbers in Zaire and Congo Brazzaville.
Organized in a powerful, centralized kingdom under the ruler, the manikongo, who ruled from the capital
Mbanza Kongo (São Salvador), the Kongo were the first
people in Angola to make contact with the Portuguese, in
1483. Initial friendly relations, which involved commercial interchange, missionaries in Kongo, and young Kongo
nobles being sent for education to Portugal, quickly
soured, especially with the development of the slave
trade in the sixteenth century. Following a crushing defeat at the hands of the Portuguese at the Battle of
Mbwila (1665), the centralized government was fatally
weakened. In the eighteenth and nineteenth centuries political authority was shared among the manikongos, provincial governors, and petty chiefs. Yet the memory of
the once-great state remained as a unifying factor and
as an inspiration in the modern political struggle.
In the twentieth century Kongo resistance to Portuguese rule was stiffened with demands for forced labor
and by land alienation. Resistance was expressed by
sporadic rebellion (e. g., 1913-14), and by a mass exodus
of refugees to Zaire. The uprising of Kongo peasants
against white settlers in March 1961, and the retaliation
of the Portuguese, was a catalyst in the Wars of Liberation that continued 1961-74. Several modern political
parties have originated in Kongo ethnonationalism, including ALIAZO, ASSOMIZO, NGWIZAKO, NTO-BAKO,
UPA, UPNA, and FNLA.

KUNZIKA, EMMANUEL MAYALA. Born 14 June 1925 at the
village of Kintoto, near Maquela do Zombo. His parents
emigrated to Belgian Congo when he was eleven, and he
was educated mainly in Léopoldville. Kunzika obtained a
managerial post in a local firm. He was also associated
with the Simão Tocoist movement.
Kunzika joined and became Vice-President of the
Zombo ethnonationalist party ALIAZO, renamed PDA in
1961. In April 1962, when the PDA joined FNLA/
GRAE, Kunzika became Vice-President. He was a mod-
erating influence, encouraging a wider Angolan repre-
sentation in the front, and especially urging toleration of
French-speaking Angolans like himself who had been

raised in Belgian Congo. He became GRAE Minister of Education and organized a primary school for children of Angolan refugees in Léopoldville. Kunzika waged a constant struggle against Roberto's dictatorial style of leadership within FNLA/GRAE, and in 1972, when Roberto purged the party ranks, he was dismissed. He retired from active politics, in 1974 completing a degree in Political Science at the National University of Zaire. See PDA.

KWANYAMA. An Ovambo subgroup. The Kwanyama kingdom of northeastern Ovamboland was the largest political entity in the Mossamedes hinterland from about 1870 to 1915. Prosperity was based on the hunting and grazing grounds of the Cuvelai flood plain, local trade in iron, copper, and salt, and long-distance trade in slaves and ivory. Under their last ruler, Mandume, the Kwanyama fiercely resisted Portuguese advance and were not finally overcome until 1915. See MANDUME; OVAMBO.

KWANZA RIVER. The Kwanza River rises in the Central Highlands and flows north and west to reach the Atlantic Ocean about 30 miles south of Luanda. The river has been important historically for several reasons: 1) the river valley has provided basic food supplies to the drier, poorer coastal regions; 2) traditionally, it has been a corridor for migration and trade to and from the coast. A line of forts along or near the river marked the advance of the Portuguese into Mbundu territory; and 3) the river is navigable as far as the Cambambe Falls, 120 miles upstream, and this is now the site of a hydroelectric scheme that provides power for the capital. See CAMBAMBE; KISAMA.

-L-

LABOR. See CONTRATADOS; FORCED LABOR; SERVIÇÃES; SLAVE TRADE.

LARA, LUCIO. Born 9 April 1929, the son of a wealthy mestiço sugar-planter from Huambo, Lúcio Lára was a founder of MPLA and remains one of its leading intellectuals. A Marxist, Lára has been a key figure in the development of the movement and of the party, especially for his work as an organizer. In the early history of MPLA he was a leader of the exile community, repre-

senting the movement at international gatherings with
others, such as Viriato da Cruz and Mário de Andrade.
In 1960 Lára opened MPLA's Conakry office, and in
1962 he was elected to the Executive Committee at the
first party conference in Léopoldville.   He became responsible for organization and for the training of cadres.
    In September 1974 Lúcio Lára was elected to
MPLA's Political Bureau and Central Committee, and in
November 1974 he led the MPLA delegation into Luanda.
Since independence Lára has maintained a low profile,
but he continues to be a key man in party organization
and policy-making.   He is the Secretary-General of
MPLA and has often been referred to as Neto's "right-
hand man. "

LIGA AFRICANA.   Founded in Lisbon in 1919 through a
    coalition of assimilados from Portuguese African col-
    onies.   For its time, its goals were radical, including
    the revocation of all discriminatory legislation.   Like
    other nationalist organizations it ran into trouble with
    the Portuguese government; its offices were closed and
    its presses shut.   In 1931 the Liga Africana was allowed
    to merge with other nationalist groups in the Movimento
    Nacionalista Africano, a government-sponsored organiza-
    tion.

LIGA ANGOLANA.   A Luanda-based organization founded in
    1912, officially approved by the government.   Its goals
    were more limited than those of the Lisbon-based Liga
    Africana, focusing on the social advancement of its
    members.   A split in 1913 led to an offshoot, the
    Grêmio Africano.   The Liga Angolana was dissolved dur-
    ing a government purge of such organizations in 1922,
    but was allowed to reform in 1929-30 in the officially
    sponsored Liga Nacional Africana.

LIGA NACIONAL AFRICANA.   Founded in 1929-30 in Luan-
    da, this was the heir to the previously purged Liga An-
    golana.   It was led mainly by Luanda-born, middle-
    class, Catholic assimilados.   If its activities and goals
    were limited by government interference, it kept alive
    the tradition of nationalist protest--through petitions, re-
    ports, literature, etc.--from the 1930s through the
    1950s.   By the latter period young, militant nationalists
    had broken away to found their own clandestine groups,
    one of which was MPLA.

LOBITO.   In 1970 Angola's third-largest city after Luanda
and Huambo; population about 60, 000.   The town was
founded in 1843 and the harbor works begun in 1903.
The completion of the Benguela Railway in 1929 was the
main stimulus to growth.   It is the Atlantic terminal for
the rail traffic from Zaire, Zambia, and Zimbabwe.
Lobito has the finest natural harbor on the Angolan coast.   A sandspit (restinga) forms a natural break-
water behind which lies a harbor 3 miles long and 1½
miles wide.   In terms of the volume of trade, Lobito is
Angola's busiest port.   It is also a growing industrial
center.

LUANDA.   The capital city of Angola; population in 1970
about half a million.
Established by Paulo Dias de Novais in 1576, Luanda was the center of the colonial administration and
the main base for Portuguese activities in Angola.   Only
once, in the period 1641-48, did Portuguese lose control
of Luanda, to the Dutch.   It was also the major slave-
trading port.
Luanda's demographic development was slow until
1940, when the population was 61, 028; since then the
population has doubled in every decade due to immigra-
tion from Europe as well as to migration of rural Africans to the city.   Luanda has also been an important
center for mestiço influence.
In the twentieth century the lower part of the city
toward the sea (baixa) was developed as a European business area, and Africans were cleared out.   They came
to live in a vast shantytown (musseques) on hills around
the city center.
Luanda has all the facilities of a major city, including an international airport; it has the main campus
of the national university (founded in 1963); it is the seat
of an archdiocese; it is linked by rail to Malanje, 200
miles to the east; it is the second seaport of Angola,
with coffee, cotton, and diamonds being the chief exports.
It is also a growing industrial center.   See MUSSEQUES.

LUBANGO (Sá da Bandeira).   The colony of Sá da Bandeira
was officially established by the Portuguese in 1885 as a
settlement for colonists from Madeira.   Situated on the
cool and healthy Huíla Plateau at an altitude of about
6, 000 feet, Sá da Bandeira was a favorite place for white
settlement, developing in the twentieth century as the
main administrative, commercial, military, educational,

and religious center of southern Angola. It has a campus of the University of Angola. Problems of communication with Mossamedes on the coast through the mountainous Chela escarpment were largely solved with the
construction of the Mossamedes Railway, which reached
Sá da Bandeira in 1923. In 1970 it was the fifth-largest city of Angola,
with a population of about 32, 000.

LUNDA, people, province. Principally located in the Shaba
region of modern Zaire, the Lunda spill over national
boundaries and are scattered through eastern Angola in
Lunda and Moxico provinces. Other Angolan groups, such as the Chokwe, Luena, Mbundu, and Ovimbundu, were influenced by Lunda
ideas and immigrants in their early history. Between
the seventeenth and nineteenth centuries the Lunda were
major purveyors of slaves to the trans-Atlantic trade.
In the nineteenth century the rapid spread of Chokwe
through eastern Angola and their conquest and colonization of Lunda areas culminated in the sacking of the
Lunda capital in 1885 and the overthrow of the paramount
ruler, the Mwata Yamvo. The intermingling of Chokwe
and Lunda peoples in this period resulted in most Lunda
of eastern Angola being heavily "Chokwe-ized." See
CHOKWE; IMBANGALA.

LUSOTROPICALISM. A theory made famous by the Brazilian
sociologist Gilberto Freyre, which held that the Portuguese were particularly adept at adapting to life in the
tropical regions and to the culture of the indigenous inhabitants of the area. Miscegenation and acculturation
were said to have produced an especially harmonious,
multiracial society in the lusophone world. The mystique
and rhetoric of lusotropicalism were much used by de-
fenders of Portuguese colonialism in the twentieth century, but the theory was much derided by Portugal's
critics.

- M -

MALANJE, town, province. Situated about 200 miles inland
from Luanda, Malanje developed in the mid-nineteenth
century as an important feira and staging post on the
route from the capital to the interior, especially to the
area of Kasanje.

Malanje is now a thriving Mbundu town with a population in 1970 of about 32, 000. The center of an important cotton- and coffee-growing area, it is linked to Luanda by rail and road.

MANDUME. Ruler of the Ovambo state of Kwanyama, 1911-17. He became a symbol of resistance to the advancing white forces in southern Angola, both Portuguese and German. Defeated by the Portuguese in 1915, Mandume fled into South-West Africa, where he was killed by a South African force in 1917.

MASSAKI, ANDRE. Born 25 February 1923 at Kikaka, Maquela do Zombo, Massaki grew up in Belgian Congo, where he was educated by Protestant missionaries. From 1942 to 1956 he worked as a clerk in commercial companies in Matadi and Léopoldville, and from 1956 to 1962 he was an editor for two publishing houses.
In December 1956 Massaki helped found ASSO-MIZO, and from 1961 to 1964 he was President of the PDA, after that time becoming the elder statesman of the party, with the title of Honorary Secretary and General Councillor. In 1962, at the formation of GRAE, Massaki was appointed Minister of Education, an office he relinquished later in the year to become President of the National Council of FNLA. This position he still held in 1972.

MASSANGANO. Situated about 110 miles from the coast east of Luanda at the confluence of the Lukala and Kwanza Rivers. A fort was established by Paulo Dias de Novais at this point in 1583 on his advance along the Kwanza against the Mbundu. Massangano was probably most important to the Portuguese in the period 1641-48, when it became the temporary capital of the colony, whilst the Dutch occupied Luanda.

MATAMBA. An eastern Mbundu kingdom situated between the Kwango and Wamba Rivers, Matamba became one of the most powerful states in the area in the mid-seventeenth century during the reign of Queen Nzinga. Together with its southern neighbor, Kasanje, it held a key position on the slave-trade routes from Lunda areas east of the Kwango to the west-coast markets. In the eighteenth and nineteenth centuries Matamba (usually called "Jinga" in contemporary sources) traders and rulers directed much of the trade to ports, such as Cabinda,

north of the Zaire River. Relations with the Portuguese
at Luanda fluctuated from periods of uneasy peace to
sporadic attempts at direct intervention by the Portuguese in Matamba affairs. It was only in the early
twentieth century that the "Jinga" were finally brought
under colonial rule. See NZINGA; SLAVE TRADE.

MBANZA KONGO (SÃO SALVADOR). Situated some 100
miles south of the Zaire River and about 200 miles from
the west coast in the Zaire district of modern Angola,
Mbanza Kongo (literally, "the city of the Kongo") was
traditionally the capital of the Kongo kingdom and the
seat of government of the manikongo. See KONGO;
ZAIRE.

MBUNDU. Language, Kimbundu. Subgroups include the Am-
bundu, Kisama, Libolo, Hako, Ndembu, Hungu, Jinga,
Mbondo, Songo, and Imbangala. The Mbundu of north-
central Angola are principally located in the districts of
Luanda, Malanje, and North and South Kwanza. They
are the second-largest ethnic group in Angola, numbering about 1.3 million.
    In the sixteenth century, at the time of the found-
ing of the Portuguese settlement at Luanda, the Mbundu
were mainly agriculturalists, craftsmen, and traders, and
were organized in small-scale centralized political systems. The impact of the Portuguese was more profound
in this region than in any other area of Angola. Economically, the major emphasis became the supply and
conveyance of slaves to coastal markets. Politically,
the intervention of the Portuguese along with the Imbangala caused the collapse of many established states, such
as Ndongo, and the development of several new kingdoms, such as Matamba, Mbondo, and Kasanje, the
prosperity of which was based on slave exports. Culturally, interaction with the Portuguese over several centuries brought the emergence of assimilados, such as
the Ambakistas. During the nineteenth century the new
demands of overseas trade for items like sugar and coffee and the expansion of colonial society brought such
problems as demands for land and labor earlier to the
Mbundu than to other Angolans.
    In the history of twentieth-century nationalism
Mbundu assimilados, particularly in Luanda, played a
key role. They provided the main ethnic base for
MPLA, and many of the present leaders of Angola, including Neto himself, are from a Mbundu background.

See AMBAKISTAS; IMBANGALA; KASANJE; MATAMBA; NDONGO.

MBWILA (AMBOUILA), BATTLE OF. Fought between Kongo and Portuguese armies on 29 October 1665, the Battle of Mbwila ended in a crushing defeat for Kongo. The manikongo, António I, was killed and his head taken back in triumph to Luanda by the Portuguese commander, Luis Lopes de Sequeira. The defeat was followed by a half-century of civil war between various claimants to the office of manikongo; the Kongo monarchy never fully recovered from this crushing blow.

MESTIÇO. A Portuguese word meaning the offspring of a racially mixed union. Mestiços have been especially influential in the history of the coastal towns of Luanda and Benguela, numbering about 8 percent of the capital's population in 1970. An important element in the colony's assimilado community, they were prominent in the liberation movements, especially in MPLA.

MINGAS, SAYDI. 13 February 1942--27 May 1977. A member of a leading Cabindan family, Saydi Mingas studied at an industrial school in Luanda and in Lisbon. He joined MPLA in the mid-1960s and had a varied career. In 1970 he studied agriculture and economic planning in Cuba and took military training; from 1971 to 1972 he directed cadres training in eastern Angola; in 1972 he was MPLA representative in Sweden.

Mingas became a member of the MPLA Central Committee in September 1974, and in January 1975 he was appointed to represent MPLA on Angola's Transitional Government as Minister of Finance and Planning. He was appointed Minister of Finance in November 1975 in Neto's first government. He served till May 1977, when he was assassinated, a victim of the abortive coup led by Nito Alves.

MIRANDA, ANTONIO JOAQUIM DE. 1864- ? Journalist and nationalist. An African assimilado, who through working as a clerk for a plantation-owner saw the ill-treatment of Africans in the recruitment process and in working conditions. He turned to journalism as a means of expressing his nationalist and republican sentiments, publishing several newspapers, A Folha de Luanda (1899), O Angolense (1907), and O Apostolado do Ben (1910). In 1908 he left his job and wrote letters to the Governor-

General protesting the abuse of African workers. For a
time he worked as a civil servant in Luanda. In 1911
he was a leader of a march to present the Governor-
General with a petition for educational reform. He was
transferred to Malanje as a tax-collector in 1912, and
in 1914 was exiled to Cabinda, accused of plotting
against the government and founding a secret society to
expel the Portuguese.

MISSIONARIES. The Portuguese considered the Catholic
   Church an essential arm of their colonial expansion.
   The Kongo ruler was baptized in 1491 and the first
   church built in Mbanza Kongo in the same year. In
   1520 an official Portuguese expedition was dispatched to
   Ndongo, one of its instructions being to convert the
   ngola to Christianity. Lack of adequate resources, high
   mortality rates among missionaries, and the varying responses of Africans meant that missionary effort could
   only be very spasmodic at best.
       The modern phase of Catholic enterprise dates
   from 1866, with the arrival of the Holy Ghost Fathers
   in Angola. Foreign Protestant missionaries were also
   active by the end of the nineteenth century. By 1920
   there were nine Protestant missions from Britain, the
   United States, Canada, Switzerland, and Germany. In
   order to avoid overlap, the main missions divided out
   their areas of interest. Thus, the Baptist Missionary
   Society, which arrived in Kongo in 1878, worked in
   northern Angola; the Methodist Church, established in
   Luanda in 1885, was active in the Mbundu area; and the
   American Board of Commissioners for Foreign Missions
   worked from 1880 in the Ovimbundu region. These religious loyalties contributed to the tripartite division of
   Angola by the three main nationalist movements.
       The major contribution of missions to Angolan de-
   velopment was in the field of education. From the arrival of the first missionaries in the fifteenth century,
   the Catholic Church promoted literacy so that its members could deal with Portuguese and Latin in church.
   And Africans were quick to appreciate the advantages of
   Western education. In the nineteenth and twentieth centuries the colonial administration virtually turned over
   elementary education to government-subsidized schools
   run by the Catholic Church. Protestant missions aimed
   to educate their members to read the Bible in their own
   language and initially promoted the vernacular, but after
   1921 the use of Portuguese in schools was made man-

datory.   After World War II the Protestant missions established scholarship programs for Angolan students to
study overseas.
        The Portuguese were always suspicious of foreign
missionaries, whom they saw as a subversive element
in Angola.   Yet the Protestant missions provided much-
needed medical services and schools, which the colonial
administration could not itself finance.

MOSSAMEDES, town, province.   Much of the province is
        semidesert.   The cold Benguela current brings a cool
        climate to the town of Mossamedes and made it a suit-
        able point for white settlement.   An expedition estab-
        lished a fort at Mossamedes in 1840, and the arrival of
        immigrants from Brazil in 1849-50 further expanded the
        settlement.   It developed as a port, a center for the
        fishing industry, and a departure point for the penetra-
        tion of southern Angola by white interests.   Communica-
        tions with the interior were much improved with the con-
        struction of a railway from Mossamedes to Lubango (Sá
        da Bandeira) and across the Huíla Plateau to Menongue
        (Serpa Pinto) some 500 miles from the coast.

MOVIMENTO POPULAR DE LIBERTAÇÃO DE ANGOLA
        (MPLA).
        1)   COLONIAL.   According to the official party
        history, MPLA was founded in December 1956 through a
        fusion of two smaller nationalist Marxist coalitions, the
        PLUA and the MIA.   In 1958 another group, the MINA,
        also joined forces.   MPLA developed as an urban-based
        movement (for example, in Luanda, Malanje, and Ben-
        guela); its main ethnic following came from the Mbundu
        areas.   It also attracted mestiço and Portuguese Marxist
        support.
        Much of the movement's internal organization was
        dismantled in 1959-60, when PIDE cracked down on Afri-
        can nationalism in Angola, arresting and imprisoning
        many leaders.   MPLA militants fought back, and the at-
        tack on the Luanda prison in February 1961 is the offi-
        cial party date for the beginning of the nationalist strug-
        gle.
        MPLA's leadership was drawn from Angolan in-
        tellectuals who had sought refuge overseas or who were
        studying abroad.   Headquarters were opened in Conakry
        (1960), Léopoldville (1961), and Brazzaville (1963).   The
        formation of the CONCP in 1961 gave MPLA a link with
        other socialist parties in Portuguese Africa.   In 1962,

at the First National Conference of MPLA in Léopoldville, Agostinho Neto, who had escaped from Portugal,
succeeded Marío de Andrade as President, a position he
held until his death.   During the period 1962-74 MPLA's party-in-exile
expanded its activities.   Guerrilla fronts were opened up
in the Dembos, Nambuangongo, Cabinda, Moxico, Cuando-
Cubango, Lunda, Malanje, Bié, and Cunene districts.
Among MPLA communities in exile and in liberated areas
of Angola, several functional organizations were active,
for example, SAM (health), CVAAR (refugees), JMPLA
(youth), OMA (women), UEA (students), UNTA (trade
unions).   Educational services and agricultural projects
were also developed.   MPLA's main source of aid was
the Soviet Union and Eastern European countries.
    A major problem at various points in MPLA's his-
tory has been factionalism caused by ideological and personal divisions.   In 1963 the defection of a group led by
Viriato da Cruz, which briefly joined GRAE, weakened
Neto's movement and was a factor in the OAU's recognition of Roberto's alliance.   Another time of weakness
for MPLA was in 1973-74, when the "Eastern Revolt"
and "Active Revolt" took place.
    A movement to consolidate the movement was
made in August-September 1974.   In August a meeting of
guerrilla leaders initiated a reorganization of MPLA's
military forces, now called FAPLA.   In September 1974
an Inter-Regional Conference of MPLA militants in Moxico appointed a thirty-five-member Central Committee and
a ten-member Political Bureau.   These were chosen from
the established leadership in exile and from among those
who had moved up through the ranks of the guerrilla
forces and other organizations during the liberation struggle.
    In November 1974 MPLA opened an office in Lu-
anda and started organizing in the urban-Mbundu areas,
where its traditional strength lay.   MPLA participated in
the Transitional Government with UNITA and FNLA, but
this broke down as fighting between the rival movements
escalated.   By July 1975 MPLA held Luanda, and control
of the capital allowed Neto to set up the new RPA there
in November 1975, with an MPLA government and a constitution drawn up by the movement.   With Cuban military
support and aid from the Soviet Union and Eastern Europe, MPLA had established its rule through much of the
country by March 1976.
    2) SINCE INDEPENDENCE.   MPLA has continued

to try to extend its influence from the urban-Mbundu
areas to accommodate rural populations of the north,
and in the central and southern plateaux. The attempted
coup by Nito Alves and his supporters in May 1977 is
seen by the party as another example of the factionalism
that has marked its history. A major issue has been the relationship between
MPLA and the people of Angola, and its role in the
country's future. In December 1977 the First Party
Congress was held, where it was resolved to turn the
liberation movement into the Angolan Workers' Party, a
Marxist-Leninist party that will spearhead the advance
of Angola toward socialism. A count of members was
instituted; membership cards were issued; party militants
will be educated in special schools; and a strict selection
procedure for membership followed. In regard to popu-
larly elected assemblies and committees, the expressions
of "people's power, " these are subordinate to MPLA Action Committees. The government itself submits to the
direction of the party Political Bureau, which is the permanent organization of the Central Committee. The party has a Secretariat and a number of departments, for
example, Administration and Finance, National Recon-
struction, Foreign Relations, Education and Culture, In-
formation/Revolutionary Orientation (DOR), Organization
(DOM), and others. See "ACTIVE REVOLT"; CONCP;
"EASTERN REVOLT"; EPLA; FAPLA; FDLA; NETO.

MOXICO. Sparsely populated province of eastern Angola that
was an important area for the operations of MPLA and
UNITA guerrillas who crossed the border from Zambia
in the late 1960s and early 1970s.

MUSSEQUES. Derived from two Kimbundu words meaning
"sandy place"; the name given to the shantytowns built on
hilly sandy grounds surrounding central Luanda. Although predominantly inhabited by Africans and mestiços
from all over Angola who came to the capital to find
work, poor whites from Portugal, Madeira, the Azores,
and elsewhere also lived in the musseques in the late
colonial period.

-N-

NAKURU AGREEMENT. As the Transitional Government
formed by the three liberation movements seemed in

67 Nascimento

danger of breaking down, African leaders persuaded
Roberto, Neto, and Savimbi to meet under the chairman-
ship of Jomo Kenyatta at Nakuru, Kenya, 16-21 June
1975. They negotiated an agreement that renounced the
use of force and outlined further plans for the transition
to independence. The agreement was almost a dead-
letter from the moment it was signed.

NASCIMENTO, LOPO FORTUNATO FERREIRA DO. Born 10
June 1942, a Mbundu from Luanda, Nascimento was educated in Luanda, completing his studies at the Vincente
Ferreira Commercial School. Nascimento was arrested
for his nationalist activities by PIDE in 1959 and 1963.
He worked as a labor organizer after his release in
1968.
    A veteran MPLA leader in Angola, Nascimento
was appointed to the party's Political Bureau and Central
Committee at the Moxico Inter-Regional Conference in
September 1974. His high standing in the movement was
shown in January 1975, when he was appointed as MPLA
representative on the Presidential Council of the Transitional Government. He became Prime Minister of the
new Angolan government in November 1975. He was
dismissed in a government reshuffle in December 1978.

NDELE, JOSE DE ASSUNÇÃO ALBERTO. Born 13 August
1940 in Cabinda, Ndele studied at a seminary in Luanda
and was a school teacher in Cabinda. For a short time
he was a member of UPA. In 1962 he went to Fribourg,
Switzerland, to study social science; after the formation
of UNITA he became active in its students' organization.
He was elected General Treasurer of UNITA at the party's Third Congress inside Angola in 1973.
    In January 1975 he was appointed as the UNITA
representative on the Presidential Council of the Transitional Government. He was also appointed as the UNITA
Prime Minister on the government of the abortive Democratic People's Republic of Angola in November 1975.

NDONGO. People and state of the Western Mbundu in the
hinterland of Luanda who came into contact with the
Portuguese colony after 1576. The demands of the slave
trade caused the Portuguese to abandon ideas of peaceful
relations, and their penetration along the Kwanza River
led to the destruction of Ndongo. Between 1612 and 1622
the Portuguese first combined with Imbangala forces to
crush the Western Mbundu state and then restored the

kingdom, putting a puppet ngola in place of the original
ruler.   In the 1660s moves by the Ndongo ruler, the
ngola Ari II, to reassert his independence caused the
Portuguese to mount another offensive.   A Portuguese
army advanced to the capital Pungu a Ndongo (Pungo
Andongo) in 1671; the ngola was killed and many of his
subjects sold in the slave trade.   The Portuguese established a new fort (presídio) at the site, marking the end
of Ndongo as even a semiindependent kingdom.

NECACA, MANUEL BARROS.   Necaca's father, Miguel Necaca, had been imprisoned for resisting the forced-labor
code in 1914.   Like many other modern Kongo leaders,
Barros Necaca (born 28 July 1914 in São Salvador) was
educated in Baptist Missionary Society schools.   From
1934 to 1937 he worked at the BMS hospital in São Salvador, and from 1937 to 1941 he trained as a medical
technician at the Currie Institute at Dondi, near Nova
Lisboa, and also in Lisbon.   Necaca also acted as the
secretary of the manikongo Pedro VII.

In 1942 Necaca moved to Léopoldville, where he
worked for a trading company.   With his young nephew
Holden Roberto he tried to mobilize support for Kongo
nationalism among the emigré community there.   He was
a principle figure in the "king palaver" in São Salvador
(1955-56) in which Kongo nationalists tried to elect a new
manikongo who would take a strong and independent stand
against Portuguese colonialism.   This move failed, and
in 1957 or thereabouts Kongo nationalists in Léopoldville
and Matadi founded a new party, the UPNA, with Necaca
as its first President.

After 1958, when the UPNA became the UPA,
Necaca lost ground to the rising young star of Kongo nationalism, Holden Roberto.   For a time Necaca was on
the Executive Council of the party, but in 1960 he quar-
reled with Roberto and resigned, although remaining
within UPA, and later FNLA.   In particular, he used
his medical knowledge in relief work for SARA among
Kongo refugees in Congo Kinshasa.   Necaca, a party
veteran, emerged from time to time to attack Roberto
for inefficiency and corruption.   In 1972 he was evicted
from SARA in a purge by Roberto of "deviationists."

NETO, ANTONIO AGOSTINHO.   Born 17 September 1922, in
Icolo-e-Bengo near Catete, Neto was doctor, poet, politi-
cian, and first President of an independent Angola.   His

father was a Methodist pastor.   Neto completed high
school at the Liceu Salvador Correia in Luanda and from
1944 to 1947 worked in the health services in the Angolan capital, at the same time acting as personal secretary to a Methodist bishop.   A scholarship enabled him
to leave for Portugal, where he studied medicine at the
universities of Coimbra and Lisbon, graduating in 1958.
During this time his antigovernment political activities
and his nationalist poetry (a book of poems was published
in 1955) resulted in his arrest and rustication, 1955-57.

In 1958 Neto returned to Angola with his Portuguese wife and opened up a medical practice.   A founder
of MPLA, Neto was soon a target for PIDE because of
his nationalist activities.   He was again arrested in June
1960 in his consulting room, an action that sparked a
protest demonstration in his village that left about thirty
dead and about 200 wounded.   In September 1960 Neto
was transferred to the Cape Verde Islands and in 1961
jailed at the Aljube prison, Lisbon.   National and international pressure led to his release, although he was
kept under house arrest.

In 1962 Neto escaped from Portugal and traveled
to Léopoldville, where he was elected President of
MPLA at its first National Conference.   From its headquarters in Brazzaville Neto directed the affairs of
MPLA during the Wars of Liberation against the Portuguese, traveling to such places as the Soviet Union,
Eastern Europe, and other African countries to solicit
support for the movement.   He was one of the founders
of the CONCP.   During the 1960s Neto also continued to
publish poetry, including the volume Sacred Hope (1963).

Neto had successfully withstood various threats to
his leadership within MPLA; for example breakaway
groups led by Viriato da Cruz, Daniel Chipenda, the
Andrade brothers, and later the coup attempt by Nito
Alves.

In September 1974 Neto presided over the MPLA
Inter-Regional Conference in the Moxico bush, where he
was appointed President of the party's Political Bureau.
During the escalating struggle of 1975 Neto was the chief
spokesperson of MPLA in the ill-fated negotiations with
UNITA and FNLA.   On 11 November 1975 Agostinho
Neto became President of the People's Republic of An-
gola.

Political commentators generally described Neto as
reserved, cautious, and a moderate.   He intended to build
a socialist state on the ruins of the old colonial system,

but his words were generally measured and freer of Marxist-Leninist rhetoric than those of his followers.   He had shown a great capacity to survive dissidence in his party, partly due to a solid circle of close followers and to his own determination and astuteness.
Neto died of cancer in the Soviet Union on 10 September 1979.

"NEW STATE" (ESTADO NOVO).   The regime in Portugal that was particularly identified with the person of António Salazar, Minister of Finance, 1928-32, and Prime Minister, 1932-68.   While briefly Minister of Colonies, he designed the 1930 Colonial Act, which included general principles for the conduct of colonial policy.   The New State rested on the three pillars of Authoritarianism, Nationalism, and Colonialism.   For Angola it meant a period of political and economic centralization; repression of nationalist activities by the police and severe censorship of the press; a division of the population into indígena and não-indígena, with education the key to assimilation; and the encouragement of white settlement, especially after World War II.   In philosophical terms, the New State elevated notions of Portugal's "civilizing missions" embodied in the theory of lusotropicalism.
See ASSIMILADO; INDIGENA; LUSOTROPICALISM.

NGANGUELA.   Important subgroups include the Luena (or Lovale), Luchazi, Ganguela, Mbuela, Mbunda.   The Nganguela constitute a heterogeneous and loosely defined population cluster.   Historically, some elements, for example, the Luena, were closely linked to the Lunda, and they were also affected by the Chokwe expansion of the nineteenth century.   Numbering about 350,000, the Nganguela are scattered through southeastern Angola in Cuando-Cubango, Moxico, and Cunene provinces.   The people are millet- and maize-growers and cattle-farmers, hunters, and fishermen, and traditionally have lived in large autonomous villages.

NGOLA A KILUANJE.   Title of the ruler of the Western Mbundu state of Ndongo, which the Portuguese encountered in the hinterland of Luanda.   Ngola was the origin of the word Angola as rendered by the Portuguese.   See NDONGO.

NKHUMBI.   Subgroups include the Humbe, Handa, and Mulondo.   Numbering about 120,000, the Nkhumbi inhabit the

widest part of the flood plain that extends on the western
side of the middle Cunene River.   They are closely related culturally and linguistically to the Nyaneka to the
northwest and the Ovambo to the southeast.   The flood
plain allows almost permanent agriculture, with cattle-
herding and plentiful hunting, which has yielded large
amounts of ivory.

By the early nineteenth century surplus production, a lively local trade, and a long-distance trade up
the Cunene River via Ovimbundu territory to Benguela
had aided the development of centralized political systems.   There was no single authority, but at its height
the kingdom of Humbe may have exercised some kind of
paramountcy over the Nkhumbi cluster.   By the second
half of the nineteenth century the rising Ovambo polity
of Kwanyama had eclipsed the Nkhumbi state.   The
Nkhumbi fiercely resisted white encroachment on their
land, and it was not until 1905 that the Portuguese completed their conquest and extended the Angola frontier to
the Cunene.

NORTON DE MATOS, JOSE MENDES RIBEIRO.   23 March
1867-1955.   Governor-General and High Commissioner
of Angola, 1912-15, 1921-24.   Born in Ponte de Lima,
Minho district, northern Portugal, from 1888 to 1890
Norton de Matos attended the Army College and was
commissioned as an officer, serving in Portuguese India
for a decade.   After 1910 his republican sympathies
gained him promotion, and in 1912 he was appointed
Governor-General of Angola.   Norton de Matos was a
powerful and energetic figure whose colonial policies
were particularly influential.

In his first term as Governor-General he attacked
residual forms of slavery and attempted to regularize the
contractual system of labor; he set up a Bureau of Native
Affairs; he initiated administrative reform, replacing
military commands with civilian administrative units; he
initiated a program of road-building and railroad and
telegraph development.

In 1921 Norton de Matos was again appointed head
of the Angolan government.   His title of High Commissioner reflected more autonomy than that of Governor-
General.   The emphasis of this administration was the
extension of Portuguese control and the unification of the
colony.   Thus, he continued the conquest of Angola especially in the eastern districts; he moved against Boer,
German, and foreign-mission influence; he ruled that

education in Portuguese was compulsory; he crushed African nationalist organizations and cracked down on freedom of the press; he encouraged white settlement as a
key to the spread of Portuguese influence. He also
sanctioned a costly public-works program, laying the
foundation of Angola's modern road network.
Norton de Matos wrote several influential books
in which he set forth his colonial philosophy: A Província de Angola (1926), Africa Nossa (1953), A Nação Una
(1953), and Memórias e Trabalhos de Minha Vida (1944-
46).

NYANEKA. Subgroups include the Huíla, Ngambwe (Gambos),
Chipungo, and Chilengue. Numbering about 140, 000, the
Nyaneka live in the Huíla Highlands of southwestern Angola. They are closely linked culturally and linguistically
with the Nkhumbi to the southeast. The Nyaneka are
farmers and herders, growing maize and practicing
transhumant pastoralism. In the mid-nineteenth century
they were divided into several small kingdoms, for example, Huíla, Njau, and Ngambwe. By the 1860s
Ngambwe was the most prominent state, its prosperity
based on the supplies of ivory it controlled in the lower
Caculovar valley. With the establishment of Sá da Bandeira and the settlement of whites on the Huíla plateau,
the Nyaneka had lost much of their best land by the end
of the nineteenth century. See HUILA; LUBANGO.

NZINGA, QUEEN OF MATAMBA. 1582(?)-1663. Ruler of
Matamba, 1624-63. A sister of the ngola of Ndongo,
Nzinga appeared in Luanda in 1621-22 as the emissary
of her brother. When he died two years later and the
Portuguese put a puppet ngola in his place, Nzinga
claimed the title and retreated eastward to Matamba to
establish her rule there. In the 1630s and 1640s she
forged an alliance with Dutch slave-traders and used her
wealth to consolidate her position. She overcame traditional Mbundu resistance to women in politics, employing
where necessary Mbundu refugees, runaway slaves, Imbangala, and others as mercenaries against local resistance. In 1656 Nzinga concluded a treaty with the
Portuguese that continued to her death. She agreed to
allow missionaries into her kingdom (having previously
converted to Catholicism herself) and permitted free
passage of slave caravans to the Kwango. See MATAM-
BA.

-O-

OIL.   Oil reserves were first located in Luanda province,
    but more recently major offshore finds have been made
    at Cabinda, Soyo (Santo António do Zaire), and the Baia
    dos Tigres in southern Angola. Oil overtook coffee as
    the top export earner in 1973. The main field in opera-
    tion at the time of independence was that of the Cabinda
    Gulf Oil Company. Whereas other major areas of the
    economy suffered disruption on account of the war be-
    tween FNLA, MPLA, and UNITA, the production of
    Cabindan oil continued relatively uninterrupted. As a
    result, in 1975-76 income from oil represented about 80
    percent of Angola's export earnings. There is a refinery
    at Luanda, and another is being built at Mossamedes.

OVAMBO (AMBO). Subgroups include the Kwanyama, Evale,
    Kafima, Kwamato, and Dombondola. The Ovambo live
    on both sides of the Angola/Namibia border. Those who
    live in Angola number about 120, 000 and are closely re-
    lated culturally and linguistically to the Nkhumbi. Living
    on the sandy plains southeast of the Cunene River on land
    that is flooded in the wet season by the Cuvelai River,
    they cultivate maize and are seminomadic cattle-herders.
         No single political authority unified the whole area,
    but several small states had emerged by the mid-nine-
    teenth century. In the second half of the century the
    Kwanyama rulers of northeast Ovamboland were one of
    the most powerful states of southern Angola. They ex-
    ploited the iron-ore deposits at Cassinga and traded with
    Walvis Bay to the south, and with the Portuguese at
    Mossamedes and Benguela, in slaves, ivory, and cattle.
    The Portuguese and Germans occupied Ovamboland in the
    face of fierce resistance between 1900 and 1917. The
    area became a backwater and a pool for migrant labor
    for the colonial economies. See KWANYAMA; NKHUMBI.

OVIMBUNDU. Language, Umbundu; important subgroups in-
    clude the Bailundu, Bieno, Dombe, Ganda, Huambo
    (Wambu), Hanha, Caconda, Chiyaka, Sambu, and Sele.
    The Ovimbundu are Angola's largest ethnic group, num-
    bering about 1. 75 million people. The name was pro-
    bably a local form of the term used by the Kongo for
    both the Mbundu and Ovimbundu who lived to the south,
    and applied freely to the latter by the Portuguese.
         Living in the fertile highlands of central Angola,
    the Ovimbundu were traditionally agriculturalists who

supplemented their diet with hunting and gathering. Salt and minerals were available in the area, and Ovimbundu men were skilled blacksmiths. They were never unified politically; by the eighteenth century twenty-two states had developed, of which three, Bailundu, Bié, and Wambu, were larger than the rest. By the late seventeenth century Portuguese traders from Benguela were in contact with the peoples of the Central Highlands, and Ovimbundu, especially from Bié, started to act as middlemen in the slave trade from the interior to the coast. By the late eighteenth and nineteenth centuries trade had become the predominant economic activity. With the decline of the northern routes from the middle Kwango area to Luanda, Ovimbundu commercial activities expanded, and traders ranged inland to the upper Zambezi and beyond for slaves, ivory, wax, dyewoods, and, at the end of the nineteenth century, wild rubber.

The late nineteenth and early twentieth centuries saw fierce resistance to the influx of Portuguese and Boer settlers into the Central Highlands, especially by the Bailundu, who saw their lands alienated and their livelihood threatened. Thousands of Ovimbundu men were forced to become migrant laborers, either moving to cities such as Nova Lisboa (Huambo), the main center of the Central Plateau region, Lobito, or Luanda, or working as contract workers on northern coffee plantations. In modern politics, the Ovimbundu have provided the main support for UNITA.

-P-

PARTIDO DEMOCRATICO ANGOLANO. Name adopted in 1961 by the Zombo alliance party, ALIAZO, in an effort to shed its ethnic image and broaden its appeal. In 1962 the PDA joined in a united front with the UPA to form GRAE. The PDA preserved its separate identity and offices and continued its own activities, for example, the organization of education and relief work among the Zombo exile community in Kinshasa and the Lower Congo. The alliance with Roberto, who treated the PDA as a useful but junior partner, was always uneasy. In 1972 Roberto purged the FNLA/GRAE leadership, ejecting several PDA leaders, such as Emmanuel Kunzika and Ferdinand Dombele. In 1973 he dissolved the PDA and

UPA and merged them in a reorganized FNLA.   See
ALIAZO; FNLA; GRAE; KUNZIKA; MASSAKI.

PARTIDO NACIONAL AFRICANO.   Founded in Lisbon in
1921, the PNA was one of several African nationalist
parties active in the metropole.   The leaders, who were
mainly mestiços and assimilados, were influenced by
current ideas of Pan-Africanism and Garveyism.   The
PNA was particularly concerned with ending forced-labor
practices and petitioned the League of Nations and the
ILO on the matter.   In 1929 branches of the party in the
colonies were banned, and under the "New State" in
1931 the PNA was merged with the Liga Africana in the
Movimento Nacionalista Africano, a reformed and government-sponsored organization.

"PEOPLE'S POWER" (PODER POPULAR).   A central theme
of MPLA's ideology has been the active participation of
the masses in the overthrow of colonialism and in the
founding and running of an independent Angola.   Article
3 of the constitution of the PRA explicitly states that
"the masses shall be guaranteed broad effective participation in the exercise of political power, through the
consolidation, expansion and development of organizational
forms of people's power. "
        Within Angola, the nascent organizations of peo-
ple's power developed first in the musseques of Luanda
as units of self-defense against white vigilante forces,
which reacted violently to the changing political climate
following the April 1974 coup in Portugal.   These
groups, which spread from the capital to other towns,
were a reservoir of support on which MPLA could draw
on its return to Luanda in November 1974.   Neighborhood
Commissions, the practical expression of people's power
in the urban areas, helped to drive FNLA and UNITA
from Luanda and to restore the daily lives of the people
in such areas as education, health, and the distribution
of food.   Committees of workers in factories and cooperatives in the countryside were other moves by the people
to organize and to get the economy moving again after
the departure of the Portuguese.
        Although the MPLA government has recognized
and worked through many of these institutions of people's
power, problems remain concerning their relationship
and the best means of incorporating the vitality and as-
pirations of these groups within a disciplined party.   See
ADMINISTRATION; MPLA.

PINNOCK, JOHNNY EDUARDO (also known as Johnny Edu-
    ardo). Born about 1942 in São Salvador, Pinnock at-
    tended elementary school in Matadi, Belgian Congo,
    where his father was station master. He later studied
    at the Institute of Political Studies, Kinshasa.
         He was early active with his father in Kongo poli-
    tics in exile. In 1960 he was a coeditor of A Voz da
    Nação Angolana, the UPA bimonthly paper; in 1962 he
    became head of the UPA youth organization and was one
    of the party representatives who signed the agreement
    founding FNLA. He represented GRAE in Algiers for a
    short time, but in 1965, after the departure of Savimbi,
    Roberto recalled Johnny Eduardo to help with the reor-
    ganization of the front and to be his chief spokesperson
    on Foreign Affairs.
         Since the early 1960s Johnny Eduardo has been
    one of Roberto's closest aides. He represented FNLA
    on the Presidential Council of the Transitional Govern-
    ment and was appointed FNLA Prime Minister of the
    Democratic People's Republic of Angola set up in opposi-
    tion to the RPA in November 1975.

PINNOCK, JOSE EDUARDO. Born 28 March 1905 at São
    Salvador, Pinnock, like many Kongo leaders, was edu-
    cated at a Baptist Missionary Society school. He even-
    tually obtained the quite senior post of railway station-
    master at Matadi.
         He became involved in Kongo politics in 1955,
    when, together with other nationalists, such as Necaca,
    he opposed the Portuguese candidate in the election of a
    new manikongo. Kongo nationalists had a candidate of
    their own whom they hoped would spearhead their cause.
         Having failed in this effort, Pinnock and others
    shifted the main center of Kongo nationalist politics to
    Léopoldville. He was a founder of UPNA/UPA and in
    1962 helped to establish FNLA. He was appointed
    GRAE's Minister of the Interior and through the 1960s
    was one of Roberto's veteran supporters. His son,
    Johnny Eduardo, became the party spokesperson for For-
    eign Affairs.

PLANALTO. Term used to refer to the savanna plateau re-
    gions of Angola, especially the central provinces of Hu-
    ambo, Bié, and Huíla, which have a healthy climate, re-
    liable rainfall, good soils, and mineral resources, and
    have therefore been a focus of population settlement, both
    African and European.

POLICIA INTERNACIONAL DE DEFESA DO ESTADO. The
International Police for the Defense of the State, better
known as PIDE, were the political police of Portugal
under the "New State. " PIDE was introduced into Angola
about 1957 as nationalist groups showed more militancy.
PIDE was used by the Portuguese administration together
with a network of informers and local officials system-
atically to root out individuals suspected of nationalist
activities. It became a byword for repression and bru-
tality and was responsible for the imprisonment and
death of hundreds of Angolan nationalists.

In 1969 the name of PIDE was officially changed
to the General Directorate of Security (DGS), but the
activities of the political police remained the same.

POMBEIRO. A word derived from pumbo, the great market
at Malebo Pool (Stanley Pool) in the area of modern
Kinshasa, frequented by Portuguese agents from the sixteenth century. The term pombeiro was used to denote
a person who traded in interior markets usually on the
account of a Portuguese merchant.

PRESIDIO. An interior fort that sometimes became the center of an administrative-military district commanded by
a military official. See ADMINISTRATION.

-R-

RAILWAYS. The railway system, developed in the colonial
period, reflects the pattern of colonization from the
coast to the interior. There are three main unconnected
lines running from west to east: 1) the Luanda Railway,
which links Luanda with Malanje; 2) the Benguela Railway, which connects Lobito and Benguela to the Zaire
and Zimbabwean railway system; and 3) the Mossamedes Railway, which serves southern Angola and
runs from Mossamedes to Lubango and terminates at
Menongue. A small fourth line, which runs about 80
miles from Porto Amboim inland to Gabela, serves a
rich coffee-, cotton-, and sisal-growing region.

RIBAS, OSCAR BENTO. Folklorist, writer. Born 17 August 1909 in Luanda, of a Portuguese father and African
mother, Ríbas was educated at the Liceu Salvador Correia. He became blind at age twenty-one and stopped
writing for about eighteen years before he returned to
novel and short-story writing.

Oscar Ríbas is a recorder of all aspects of
Mbundu and Afro-Portuguese culture, from folktales to
religion and the culinary arts, and these he has incorporated into his prose writing. While influencing a new
generation of Angolan writers, he is not generally accepted by them because of the ambivalence of his attitudes to indigenous culture, which may reflect the am-
biguities of his Afro-Portuguese background. Whilst
striving to communicate the authenticity of the Angolan
heritage, he at times derides the culture and compares
it unfavorably with that of the Portuguese. Apart from
his prose fiction, Ríbas has also published collections of
folktales.

ROBERTO, HOLDEN ALVARO. Born 12 January 1923 in
São Salvador, Holden Roberto has lived most of his life
outside of Angola in the Kongo exile and emigré community in Zaire. At age two he moved with his aunt to
Léopoldville, where he was educated in a Baptist Missionary Society school between 1925 and 1940. In 1940-
41 he was sent back to the mission school in São Salvador
for a year to improve his Portuguese. He then worked
for eight years as a clerk in the Belgian Congo Provincial Administration in Léopoldville, Bukavu, and Stanley-
ville. From 1949 to 1957 he had a job alongside his
uncle, Barros Necaca, at the Nogueira Trading Company
in Léopoldville.

It was during this time that Roberto came under
the influence of Kongo nationalists both in Congo and in
northern Angola. He became involved in the nascent liberation movement and in 1958 was sent as a delegate of
the newly formed UPNA to the All-African Peoples Conference in Accra. There he saw the need to broaden the
base of his party from Kongo nationalism to Angolan nationalism, and he instigated the name-change from
UPNA to UPA. In 1959 he became attached to the
Guinea United Nations delegation and presented the case
of Angolan nationalists before the world assembly in New
York. He also wrote articles publicizing the Angolan
situation and attended various international and African
congresses. On his return in 1960 to Léopoldville,
where UPA had opened an office, Roberto established
himself as party President, after a power struggle with
veterans in the Kongo nationalist movement. Since this
time he has survived all challenges to his leadership.

Holden Roberto has tried at various points to
broaden the base of his party's support. At times he

attracted several non-Kongo politicians into the party
leadership, but basically his mass following has been
among the Kongo. In 1962 he negotiated and concluded
the merger of the PDA with his UPA in the FNLA, of
which he has been President ever since. In April 1962
he established GRAE, mainly formed by UPA members,
and his greatest political victory over his rival Neto and
the MPLA was the recognition of GRAE by the OAU in
1963. One of Roberto's political strengths has been the
support he has received from his brother-in-law, President Mobutu of Zaire.

Following the Portuguese coup in 1974 Roberto
negotiated the entry of FNLA into Luanda in November
1974, but he never ventured into the MPLA/Mbundu
stronghold himself. In January 1975 he signed the Alvor
Agreement with Portugal, MPLA, and UNITA initiating
the Transitional Government. In July 1975, after an almost lifelong exile, Roberto returned to northern Angola
to direct the war against MPLA. He negotiated the
formation of a government with Savimbi in opposition to
the RPA, in November 1975. Following the military
victory of MPLA in March 1976, FNLA and Roberto retreated from Angola back to their bases in Zaire. Since
then Roberto has lived quietly in Kinshasa directing low-
level guerrilla operations against MPLA in northern Angola and trying to solicit international support for his
organization. See FNLA; GRAE; NECACA; PDA; UPA;
UPNA.

ROCHA, CARLOS (DILOLWA). Born about 1940, and an
MPLA militant since the late 1950s, Rocha has been one
of the movement's leading Marxist mestiço intellectuals.
In the mid-1960s he was an instructor of MPLA guerrillas in Congo Brazzaville, and in 1969 he directed the
regional Center for Revolutionary Instruction in Eastern
Bié. He also, for a time, edited the movement's journal Vitória Certa.

Rocha's emergence as a member of MPLA's
leadership was signaled at the conference of party mili-
tants in Moxico in September 1974. He was then ap-
pointed to the Political Bureau and Central Committee.
One of Neto's closest advisors, he became Minister of
Planning and Finance in the first RPA government in
November 1975 and helped lay plans for national recon-
struction. In November 1976 Rocha was made Second
Deputy Prime Minister and Secretary of the National
Planning Commission. He was also Chairman of the
Angolan-Cuban Commission.

In a government shake-up in December 1978
Carlos Rocha was dismissed from his position as Deputy
Premier and from the Political Bureau and Central
Committee of MPLA.

-S-

SANGUMBA, JORGE ISAAC. Born 7 October 1944, an Ovimbundu and son of a Protestant male nurse at Bailundo
near Nova Lisboa, Sangumba and his parents moved in
1948 to Cabinda, where he began his education. He attended secondary schools at Malanje, 1955-61, and at
Nova Lisboa, 1961-63.
    Sangumba at first worked for MPLA distributing
pamphlets. Forced into exile at age eighteen, he made
his way via Rhodesia to Dar es Salaam, where he met
Eduardo Mondlane, who arranged a scholarship for him
to study in the United States. He attended Lincoln University, Pennsylvania, and Manhattan College, New
York, from 1964 to 1968 and graduated with a degree
in political science.
    After meeting Savimbi in Cairo in 1968, Sangum-
ba joined UNITA and traveled as a party envoy in several African countries. In 1969 he was named Foreign
Minister. From 1970 to 1972 he served also as party
representative in London and edited the UNITA magazine
Kwacha Angola. Whilst in the English capital he gained
a diploma in international affairs from the University of
London.
    Since Angolan independence Jorge Sangumba has
remained one of Savimbi's closest advisors and the party
spokesperson on foreign policy. He travels widely
soliciting international support for UNITA.

SANTOS, JOSE EDUARDO DOS. Born 28 August 1942 in
Luanda. Santos became an active member of the
JMPLA at age nineteen. He enlisted in MPLA's guerrilla army in 1962. An excellent student, he was sent
to study in the Soviet Union on an MPLA scholarship,
1963-70, and graduated with degrees in petroleum engineering and radar telecommunications.
    Santos served as MPLA representative in Yugo-
slavia and for a time was head of the Brazzaville office.
In September 1974 he was appointed to the MPLA Central Committee and ranked fifth on the Political Bureau.
He served as Foreign Minister in the first RPA govern-

ment, and then as First Vice Prime Minister. In the
government reshuffle of December 1978 he was dismissed, but a few days later was given the important
post of Minister of National Planning and also served as
the party Secretary for Economic Development and Planning.
    At age thirty-seven José Eduardo dos Santos was
appointed to succeed Agostinho Neto as President of Angola. He was sworn into office on 21 September 1979.
Politically, he is considered to be pragmatic and a party
moderate.

SAVIMBI, JONAS MALHEIROS. Born 3 August 1934 at Mun-
hango, Moxico, where his father was an employee on the
Benguela Railway, Savimbi attended the Protestant primary school at his father's village, Chilesso, near An-
dulo in Bié province. He was also educated at the
Dondi Mission School and in secondary schools in Silva
Porto and Sá da Bandeira.
    In September 1958 he was awarded a scholarship
by the United Church of Christ to study medicine at the
University of Lisbon. In 1960 he transferred to Fribourg University and then to the University of Lausanne,
Switzerland, where he studied political science.
    A meeting with the Kenyan nationalist leader Tom
Mboya at a students' conference in Kampala in 1961 con-
vinced Savimbi to enter politics full-time. In the same
year he joined the UPA, becoming its General-Secretary.
He was the first Ovimbundu to be given a major position
in Roberto's party. With Roberto, he played a key role
in negotiating the alliance of the PDA and the UPA and
in the creation of FNLA/GRAE. In April 1962 he was
appointed Foreign Minister of the government-in-exile.
    Disillusioned with Roberto and his leadership,
Savimbi and other Ovimbundu broke with FNLA/GRAE
in 1964 and formed a new group, AMANGOLA, a move
that culminated in March 1966 in the founding of UNITA
inside Angola. From July 1968 to April 1974, Savimbi
went underground, organizing UNITA political, educational, and military activities in eastern and southern
Angola, and leaving much of the marshaling of external
support to other UNITA representatives, such as Sangumba.
    A first-rate orator and charismatic leader, Sav-
imbi came into his own after he concluded a cease-fire
between Portugal and UNITA in June 1974. He moved
into southern and central Angola, mobilizing support for

his party and allaying the fears of Angola's white community, whom he impressed by his moderation. With Portugal, Neto, and Roberto, he concluded the Alvor Agreement in January 1975, and traveled widely in Angola rallying support for UNITA. His uneasy alliance with Roberto in the establishment of a government in opposition to Neto in November 1975 was short-lived. Since the military defeat of UNITA, Savimbi has again gone underground in the bush of southeastern Angola with UNITA forces, directing guerrilla activities against the MPLA regime, and leaving much of the international lobbying on behalf of UNITA to other party representatives. See AMANGOLA; UNITA.

SERPA PINTO. Town of southeastern Angola. Renamed Menongue, this is the administrative center of Cuando-Cubango province and the inland terminal of the Mossamedes Railway.

SERPA PINTO, ALEXANDRE ALBERTO DA ROCHA DE. 20 April 1846--28 December 1900. Portuguese explorer, soldier, and colonial administrator. His most famous journey was in 1877-79, when he set out from Benguela, traveled east to the Zambezi, and finally reached the southeast African coast at Durban in South Africa. This trans-African journey was greeted with great enthusiasm in Portugal. It galvanized support for African ventures and gave impetus to the á contra costa scheme--a coast-to-coast Portuguese colony--which was later dropped because of British opposition. Serpa Pinto also served as Portuguese consul in Zanzibar in 1887 and in 1889 was Governor-General of Mozambique. His book How I Crossed Africa was translated into French, German, and English in 1881 and was widely read.

SERTANEJO. A Portuguese word meaning a person of the backcountry, used in Angola, especially in the nineteenth century, to refer to a European trader-settler of the interior plateau regions.

SERTÃO. A Portuguese word meaning interior or hinterland, sertão is commonly used in Angola and Brazil to refer to the inland regions.

SERVIÇÃES (lit. a servant). Often used in the Angolan context in the late nineteenth and early twentieth centuries as a euphemism for forced laborers, for example, those

traded to work on the plantations of São Tomé and Príncipe.

SETTLERS. In spite of the continuous Portuguese presence
in Angola since 1483, there was very little permanent
white settlement before the twentieth century. Most
Europeans were either temporary residents, such as administrators, soldiers, and missionaries, or exiled
criminals (degredados). In 1900 the white population
numbered about 9, 200 and was concentrated in the coastal
towns of Luanda, Benguela, and Mossamedes.
    In the twentieth century, and especially after the
Second World War, the Portuguese government intervened
to encourage emigration to Angola, offering incentives to
agricultural settlers--in particular, free transportation,
land, housing, animals, and subsidies. This policy was
aimed at resettling impoverished peasants from Portuguese rural areas and at extending European influence in
the interior of Angola. Thus, the white population increased from 44, 083 in 1940 to 172, 529 in 1960, and to
about 335, 000 in 1974. Efforts to settle white immigrants in planned agricultural settlements (colonatos)
largely ended in failure. Most Portuguese settlers came
from illiterate, rural backgrounds and had ambitions
about entering the commercial sector, usually as small
traders. Many moved to the towns taking jobs that
might otherwise have been filled by Africans.
    In 1975, on the eve of Angolan independence, as
many as 90 percent of Angola's white settlers and expatriates left the country, causing massive disruption in
the economy. Those who chose to return to Portugal
were known as the retornados. Since independence the
MPLA government has started the screening and repatri-
ation of those who wish to return to Angola.

SILVA PORTO. The capital of Bié province, and renamed
    Bié. See BIE.

SILVA PORTO, ANTONIO FRANCISCO DA SILVA. 24 Au-
    gust 1817--1 April 1890. Born in Porto, Portugal, and
    generally known as Silva Porto. He went to Brazil at
    age twelve and in 1838 settled in Angola, first at Luanda
    and Benguela; in 1845 he built a homestead at Belmont,
    Bié. As a settler, backwoodsman, and trader, Silva
    Porto was one of the most famous sertanejos of Angola
    in the nineteenth century. He traveled widely in the re-
    gion between Benguela and the Upper Zambezi, aiding

European explorers, such as Cameron, Serpa Pinto, Ivens, and Capelo, and missionaries, such as Livingstone and Arnot. He attempted a trans-African journey in 1852-54, but was stopped by illness in Lozi territory, although his pombeiros reached the Mozambique coast. Silva Porto became increasingly concerned and embittered by growing foreign infiltration in Central Africa and Portugal's apparent weakness. He was the Portuguese representative in Bié, 1885-90, and urged Lisbon to act to secure Angola as a colony. He committed suicide in 1890. Edited extracts from his journals and letters have been published.

SLAVE TRADE. Approximately 4 million slaves were exported from the Angola-Congo region (between Cape Lopez and Cape Frio) in the trans-Atlantic slave trade, c. 1500--c. 1870. Several phases can be distinguished. Initially it was a demand from São Tomé traders and planters that stimulated the Angolan trade. Slaves were exported from the Kongo kingdom through the port of Mpinda on the south side of the Zaire estuary. With the expansion of Brazil's economy, the Kongo area was unable to satisfy the demand for labor, and São Tomé and Portuguese traders shifted the focus of their activities to Mbundu territory. An official slave trade was established from Luanda after 1576, and in the seventeenth century Portuguese administrators extended their control over the Bengo-Kwanza region, sending agents inland to establish feiras for slave-trading purposes. By the late seventeenth century the broad outlines of the pattern of trading that continued into the nineteenth century were set. The main official trade was through Mbundu territory to the states of the middle Kwango region, Matamba and Kasanje, which traded in Lunda territory further east. A southern route was developed by pombeiros from Benguela to Ovimbundu territory and beyond. A serious threat to the official Portuguese trade was a northern route from the Middle Kwango through Kongo territory to ports, such as Cabinda, north of the Zaire River, where Dutch, English, and French traders predominated. In the eighteenth century the slave trade was the basis of the economy of the colony of Angola.

The Angolan slave trade was officially abolished by the Portuguese government in 1836, but it was carried on as long as the demand from Brazil and São Tomé continued. Even in the twentieth century the legacy

of centuries of slave-trading remained, as forced labor
was seen by white Angolans as the remedy for labor
shortages.

SOBA. Local African chiefs recognized by the Portuguese
in return for their collaboration. Sobas sometimes, but
by no means always, derived from traditional ruling
families, but their power rested on Portuguese recognition and support. The Luanda administration had neither
the money nor the manpower to extend and consolidate
its influence in the interior without alliances with the
sobas, who supplied soldiers and porters, and procured
foodstuffs and trade goods for the Portuguese. See
ADMINISTRATION.

SOROMENHO, FERNANDO MONTEIRO DE CASTRO. 31
January 1910--18 June 1968. Short-story writer and
novelist. Born of European parents in Mozambique,
Soromenho and his family moved to Angola in 1911. He
was sent to primary and secondary school in Portugal,
but in 1925 returned to Angola, where he worked for
Diamang, and later as a civil servant and a journalist.
In 1937 he returned to Lisbon to start his own publishing
house, Edições Sul. Forced to close his business by
the authorities, he fled to France in 1960. He died in
exile in Brazil in 1968.

Soromenho was one of the first Portuguese writers to move away from an exotic approach in his por-
trayal of African society, and to attempt to present it as
it really was for Portuguese readers. He wrote from a
belief in the common humanity of people, their experiences and emotions, regardless of ethnic origins. Several of his stories are set in eastern Angola, an area
with which he was particularly familiar. Soromenho's
early writings nevertheless betray an ethnocentricism
and paternalism, attitudes that drew criticism from later
nationalist writers. He is most successful when dealing
with colonial situations of social transition and culture
conflict.

SOUSA COUTINHO, FRANCISCO DE INOCENCIO DE. Governor-General of Angola, 1764-72. One of the few vi-
sionary Governors of Angola, Sousa Coutinho saw the
need to make the colony more than a source of slaves
for Brazil. He attempted to promote internal development through such measures as sponsoring the settlement
of the Benguela plateau by European colonists; encourag-

ing local agriculture; starting a shipyard, an iron found-
ry, and leather and soap factories.   He founded a
school for engineers in Luanda and a chamber of commerce for traders.   Most of his far-sighted policies
lapsed after his departure, but the example of what he
had accomplished remained.

SOYO. Known in the colonial period as Santo António do
    Zaire, the modern name derives from the Soyo (Sonyo,
    Sohio) province of the Kongo kingdom. Occupying a key
    position on the southern side of the Zaire estuary and
    along the Atlantic Coast to the south, Soyo was the first
    area of Angola reached by Portuguese ships when they
    arrived at Mpinda (near the site of the modern town of
    Soyo) in 1483. The Solongo, the Kongo subgroup that
    inhabits the region, were major suppliers of slaves to
    traders from São Tomé and Portugal before the estab-
    lishment of the Luanda and Mbundu trade.
        The modern town of Soyo is of growing importance
    because of large reserves of offshore oil, which have
    not yet been fully exploited.

-T-

TOCO, SIMÃO GONCALVES. Religious leader. Born 24
    February 1918 at Sadi Kiloango, a village near Maquela
    do Zombo, Toco attended the Baptist Missionary Society
    school at Kibokolo, 1926-33, and the Liceu Salvador
    Correia in Luanda, 1933-36. From 1937 to 1943 he
    taught at mission schools in Kobokolo and Bembe. In
    1943 he moved to Léopoldville, where he helped to or-
    ganize mutual-aid groups among Zombo emigrés and di-
    rected the choir of the Baptist Mission church. During
    this time he was much influenced by the teachings of the
    Kimbanguist and Watch Tower churches, especially by
    ideas on millennialism.
        In 1949 he and some followers believed they had
    a vision to form their own church, led by Simão Toco,
    the prophet, and twelve Apostles appointed by him. They
    preached separation from white society, a puritanical
    lifestyle, and the virtues of self-reliant behavior. As
    with many prophet-churches of the colonial period, the
    Tocoist movement came to be seen by the Belgian and
    Portuguese authorities as a focus of black, nationalist
    sentiment and a threat to the colonial regime. In fact,
    Toco advocated African personal and social reform and

rejection of white society, not political action against it.
In December 1949 he and other Tocoist leaders
in Congo were arrested by the Belgians and handed over
to the Angolan authorities. He was detained by the
Portuguese in several camps before being sent into iso-
lation through his appointment as lighthouse keeper at
Ponta Albina, near Porto Alexandre, 1955-62.

Released briefly, in 1962 he traveled in northern
Angola, urging his followers to come out of hiding and
settle in Portuguese resettlement villages. In 1963,
still viewed as a potential political threat, he was exiled
in the Azores, but the church that he had established in
Angola lived on.

TRANSITIONAL GOVERNMENT. Set up by Portugal and the
three liberation movements in the Alvor Agreement on
15 January 1975, the Transitional Government was given
the responsibility of governing Angola from 31 January
1975 until independence on 11 November 1975. In particular it was to draft a provisional constitution and conduct legislative elections. The Transitional Government
was headed by a Portuguese High Commissioner and had
a premiership which rotated among the three liberation movements. There was a twelve-member Cabinet,
with Portugal and the three African parties each holding
three ministries. Each liberation movement contributed
8, 000 troops to an integrated army, together with 24, 000
Portuguese troops.

The Transitional Government collapsed in July
1975 after fighting between the three liberation movements made peaceful cooperation impossible. In August
1975 Portugal formally dissolved the defunct Transitional
Government.

- U-

UIGE, town, province. Important coffee-growing region of
northeastern Angola, with the administrative and commercial capital at Uige (previously named Carmona).
Following peasant uprisings against white settlers in
March 1961 and the overreaction of Portuguese militia
and civilians, thousands of Kongo refugees left the area
and fled to Zaire. Uige, together with the neighboring
province of Zaire, was the main operation area for
UPA/FNLA guerrillas, 1961-74. From 1974 to 1976
Uige and the town of Carmona were the center of FNLA
activities in Angola during the civil war.

UNIÃO DAS POPULAÇÕES DE ANGOLA. In 1958 the UPNA,
at the initiative of Holden Roberto, changed its name to
the UPA in order to broaden its political base from
parochial Kongo nationalism to Angolan nationalism. Its
main external office was in Léopoldville. Congo independence in 1960 stimulated UPA to increase its organizational and propaganda drive. After the uprising by
Kongo peasants against white settlers in northern Angola
in March 1961 UPA started to coordinate a guerrilla
war against the Portuguese. A guerrilla army and several functional bodies, including a trade-union affiliate
(LGTA), a youth movement (JUPA), and a medical organization to aid refugees (SARA), were organized. By
1962 the UPA had also started to establish a rudimentary
system of self-government in areas of northern Angola
under its control. In 1962 the UPA under Holden
Roberto allied itself to the PDA to form a common front,
FNLA/GRAE. See FNLA; GRAE; UPNA.

UNIÃO DAS POPULAÇÕES DO NORTE DE ANGOLA. A
Kongo nationalist party founded about 1957 (some sources
claim 1954) by Kongo emigrés in Léopoldville and Matadi. This was an attempt to broaden the base of Kongo
nationalism, which had previously been focused on the
revival of the old Kongo kingdom.
     In 1958 UPNA sympathizers financed a mission
by Holden Roberto to the All-African Peoples' Conference in Accra, Ghana. Roberto then changed the name
of the party to the UPA. See UPA.

UNIÃO NACIONAL PARA A INDEPENDÊNCIA TOTAL DE
ANGOLA (UNITA). Following his break with Holden
Roberto and the FNLA in December 1964 Jonas Savimbi
moved to Lusaka, where he drew three main elements
together in a new liberation front--ex-GRAE defectors
like himself, most of whom were Ovimbundu and had
previously grouped together in the AMANGOLA; Angolan
students abroad (UNEA); and Angolan refugees in Zambia
and members of former Chokwe, Luena, and Luchazi
self-help associations in Lusaka. Savimbi thus based
his party on support from the Ovimbundu, the largest
ethnic group of Angola, and from other rural populations
of eastern and southern Angola.
     The founding of UNITA dates from a meeting at
Muangai in Moxico district, some 250 miles west of the
Zambian border in March 1966. Socialism, self-reli-
ance, and the need to continue the struggle inside Angola

were constant themes. At a follow-up congress in September 1966 a Central Committee was elected.

In December 1966 UNITA guerrillas opened up an Eastern Front with an attack on the Benguela Railway near Teixera de Sousa. The railway, which carries Zambian copper to the Atlantic port of Lobito, was temporarily cut, and in retaliation Zambia exiled Savimbi and UNITA, leaving them without an external base contiguous with Angola. After a short stay in Egypt, Savimbi returned to Angola in June 1968, remaining underground inside the country until April 1974.

During the period of the liberation struggle against the Portuguese, UNITA was militarily the weakest of the three movements. It had little external structure apart from its London office and did not have functional organizations like FNLA or MPLA. It lacked any major external source of arms, receiving only a modest supply of weapons from China. UNITA retained a low profile and concentrated on constructing and educating a self-reliant political underground inside Angola.

In June 1974, following a cease-fire with Portugal, UNITA moved into the Central Highlands, its natural political stronghold. In January 1975 UNITA joined with Portugal, FNLA, and MPLA in the Transitional Government. At the same time Jonas Savimbi, a most effective and charismatic leader, traveled widely in Angola and outside, soliciting support for his party. He was particularly successful in calming the fears and winning the support of Angola's European community. As the civil war escalated in 1975 Savimbi had to seek out external support and turned to South Africa, a move that damned him and his party in the eyes of many, particularly in the rest of Africa. His attempt in November 1975 to form a coalition with Roberto, in opposition to the RPA, failed, and by March 1976 UNITA had lost the war to MPLA and the Cubans.

Since March 1976 Savimbi and UNITA have gone underground in eastern and southeastern Angola, mainly in Bié, Moxico, and Cuando-Cubango provinces, from where they operate a low-level guerrilla activity against the MPLA government. UNITA was expelled from Zaire and Zambia and thus continued to depend on South Africa, through Namibia, for its main external base. See AMANGOLA; SAVIMBI.

-V-

VIEIRA, JOSE LUANDINO.   Short-story writer and novelist.
Born in 1935 in Portugal, José Vieira Mateus de Graça
is better known by his pseudonym, Luandino Vieira.   He
was taken to Angola at age three and has spent most of
his life there.   He was arrested by the colonial authorities and imprisoned for his nationalist activities, 1961-
72.   For much of this time he was detained in a penal
camp in the Cape Verde Islands.   He was conditionally
released in 1972 and was in Lisbon at the time of the
coup in April 1974.   On his return to Luanda he was appointed Director of Programs for the People's Television
of Angola.   He helped to found the Union of Angolan
Writers and became Director of MPLA's Department of
Revolutionary Orientation.
     Luandino Vieira is one of Angola's best-known
and most popular writers.   His views on national liberation and social reform are exemplified in several works.
His best-known book is a collection of three long short
stories entitled Luuanda (1964).   For this he was awarded
the Portuguese Writers Society award for prose fiction
in 1965.   However, the author was in prison, and the
book was banned as subversive by the Portuguese authorities.

-Z-

ZAIRE, river, province.   Angola's only direct access to the
Zaire River is for a distance of 93 miles from the
Atlantic Coast to Noki.   Here the river forms the northern boundary between Angola and the country of Zaire.
     The northwestern province of Angola, also called
Zaire, has its administrative center at the old capital of
the Kongo kingdom, Mbanza Kongo (known in the colonial
period as São Salvador).   Zaire province is a major
palm-oil- and coffee-producing region and has important
offshore oil reserves at the coastal town of Soyo.   As
with the neighboring province of Uige, much of the local
Kongo population of Zaire fled as refugees to the country
of Zaire during the latter part of the colonial period.

BIBLIOGRAPHY

TABLE OF CONTENTS

VIII. CULTURAL

I.   INTRODUCTION

In the past two decades or so English-speaking scholars have
been increasingly involved with Angolan studies, and some
disciplines, of which history is one, are quite well served
with works in English.   A good knowledge of Portuguese remains an essential prerequisite for any serious study of the
country, however.   This is especially true once the research-
er goes beyond the secondary sources; French and German
are also frequently necessary.   Since the African Historical
Dictionaries are primarily intended for English-speakers,
works in English, even those of less importance, are given
emphasis in this bibliography.   Only the main works in Portuguese and other languages are cited.   Where English trans-
lations exist, these are listed in preference to the original.
History and politics are the focus of the bibliography; other
disciplines receive less attention, and the bibliography does
not claim to be complete.   Studies of Angola appear not only
as specific articles or monographs on the country itself, but
are also found in collections on lusophone Africa, Southern
Africa, and Central Africa.

It is not always easy to keep abreast of affairs in Angola.
Most of the other countries with which this series is concerned have been independent for fifteen years or more.   At
the time of writing Angolan independence is only four years
old.   In this short time many changes have taken place both
in Angola and also in Portugal, following the coup of 1974.
Transformations have been wrought not only in political, economic, and social affairs, but also in terms of research organizations and publications.   Many of the institutions that
published research in Portugal and Angola in the pre-1974-75
period have been abolished or are in the process of being
restructured.

In general, the English-language media in the United States
and Europe seldom give any news coverage of Angola, unless
there are events of international significance, such as the

wars that accompanied independence and the Soviet and Cuban involvement in the area. These happenings may be reported in such newspapers as the Christian Science Monitor, the Washington Post, the New York Times, and in the foreign press, for example, the Times and Observer (London) and Le Monde (Paris). Of some help are the weekly AF Press Clips (AF/P Room 3509, Department of State, Washington, DC, 20520) which contain reports on Africa, mainly collected from English-language newspapers. Articles on Angola are occasionally included in such publications as West Africa (London, weekly), Africa Report (African-American Institute, New York, bimonthly), and Africa Confidential (London, bi-weekly).

One of the best sources of current news is the fortnightly Facts and Reports: Press Cuttings on Southern Africa (Holland Committee on Southern Africa, Da Costastraat 88, Amsterdam, Holland). This publishes press cuttings on Southern Africa taken from the international news media (and frequently translated into English), including Angolan and Portuguese newspapers reports, and articles printed in other African and European countries. On economic affairs, a useful publication is the Economic Review for Angola and Mozambique (Economist Intelligence Unit, London; annual and quarterly). Since 1977, the Department of Revolutionary Orientation (C. P. 3205, Luanda, Angola) has published an Information Bulletin in English (No. 1, April 1977), which includes official MPLA statements and a summary of events.

Several organizations exist to publish and disseminate information on Angola, for example, the Liberation Support Movement, P. O. Box 2077, Oakland, CA 14604; the Mozambique, Angola, and Guiné Information Centre (MAGIC), 34 Percy Street, London W1P 9FG; and the Africa Fund (associated with the American Committee on Africa), 305 East 46th Street, New York, NY 10017. The International Conference Group on Modern Portugal, c/o Professor Douglas Wheeler, Department of History, University of New Hampshire, Durham, NH 03824, promotes the exchange of information on research activities between scholars interested in Portugal and Portuguese-speaking Africa.

History and Politics

For many years the only general surveys of Angolan history in English were those of James Duffy, Portuguese Africa (Cambridge: Harvard University Press, 1959) and Portugal

in Africa (Harmondsworth, Middlesex: Penguin, 1962), and
these volumes are still well worth reading. In the mid-
1960s Angolan history was treated in the broader context of
Central African history in Jan Vansina, Kingdoms of the
Savanna (Madison: University of Wisconsin Press, 1966),
and in the context of the lusophone countries of Africa in
Ronald H. Chilcote, Portuguese Africa (Englewood Cliffs,
N. J.: Prentice-Hall, 1967). A useful general survey of
Angolan history that deals with the period from the late fif-
teenth century is that of Douglas Wheeler and René Pélissier,
Angola (New York: Praeger, 1971; reprint Greenwood Press,
1978).

The long and enduring contacts between Portugal and Angola
have been the subject of several articles and books written
by the doyen of the study of Portuguese overseas expansion,
Charles Boxer. His works include Race Relations in the
Portuguese Empire (Oxford: Clarendon Press, 1963), Portuguese Society in the Tropics (Madison: University of Wisconsin Press, 1965), and The Portuguese Seaborne Empire
(London: Hutchinson, 1969). Another succinct overview of
the problem is that of David Birmingham, The Portuguese
Conquest of Angola (London: Institute of Race Relations, Ox-
ford University Press, 1965). Portuguese imperialism in
Africa in the nineteenth century has been explored at length
in several studies by Richard Hammond, including Portugal
and Africa 1815-1910 (Stanford, Calif.: Stanford University
Press, 1966). An important and stimulating overview of
Portuguese rule in Angola is the recent work by Gerald
Bender, Angola Under the Portuguese: The Myth and Reality
(Berkeley: University of California Press, 1978).

The slave trade and the use of forced labor are important
themes in Angolan historiography. Basil Davidson's Black
Mother (London: Gollancz, 1961) is an early classic in the
field. In the last decade or so, however, new research
techniques have allowed a much more precise analysis of the
trans-Atlantic trade. Of these newer studies, those by Herbert Klein (1969, 1972, 1975, 1978) and Joseph Miller (1975,
1976) are particularly noteworthy. Portuguese forced-labor
policies in the twentieth century have also been the subject
of several books, for example, the synthesis of James Duffy,
A Question of Slavery (Oxford: Clarendon Press, 1967).

Another important topic that has received some attention is
the growth of Angolan nationalism. Douglas Wheeler has
published several works (1968, 1969, 1970, 1972) on the nature of African responses to Portuguese colonialism in the

nineteenth century, whilst René Pélissier's massive two volumes, Les Guerres Grises and La Colonie du Minotaure
(Montamets, France: Pélissier, 1977 and 1978), will long
remain indispensable reading for the history of Angolan resistance.   The explosion of African nationalism in 1961 and
the ensuing guerrilla struggle signaled a great outpouring of
literature, most of which was heavily biased in favor of one
or all of the liberation movements involved, or in support of
Portuguese policies.   By far the most important and balanced
survey of this theme is that of John Marcum, The Angolan
Revolution (2 volumes; Cambridge: MIT Press, 1969 and
1978).   The notes and bibliographies of these two books are
also a mine of information on the period, its personalities,
and the literature.

Angolan independence has been so recent that few works, at
least in English, have appeared as yet on the post-1975 period.   Africa Contemporary Record: Annual Survey and Documents, edited by Colin Legum (New York: Africana), has
contained some useful surveys of events, whilst the magazine
published by MAGIC, People's Power in Mozambique, Angola
and Guinea Bissau (1976-   ), usually sympathetic to the new
governments, contains analysis of the postindependence period.   Øle Gjerstad's The People in Power (Oakland: LSM
Press, 1976), is a first-hand account of events in Angola
just after independence and is especially interesting for its
description of the workings of "people's power. "

Anthropology, Sociology, and Culture

Compared to the fields of history and politics, few works in
English have appeared on the above topics.   In anthropology,
students of the Kikongo-speaking peoples of northern Angola
have benefited from the study of Wyatt MacGaffey, Custom
and Government in the Lower Congo (Berkeley: University
of California Press, 1970).   Although based on research on
the Zaire side of the border, MacGaffey's findings are rele-
vant for the Kongo of Angola.   The numerous Ovimbundu
people of central Angola were the subject of several early
studies (Hambly, 1934; Childs, 1949; McCulloch, 1952; and
Edwards, 1962); however, these are now a bit dated and new
research needs to be undertaken.   For southern Angola, the
important work of Carlos Estermann is now being made ac-
cessible through the translation into English of his The Ethnography of Southwestern Angola Vol. I and II (New York:
Africana, 1976 and 1979) by Gordon Gibson.

In the field of sociology the most significant volume is the collection of essays edited by the German scholar Franz-Wilhelm Heimer, Social Change in Angola (Munich: Weltforum Verlag, 1973), which has several interesting contributions and also points the way to lines of future inquiry.

Finally, in the study of Angolan literature, mention must be made of the pioneering work of Gerald Moser (1962, 1969, 1970) and to the excellent overview published by Russell Hamilton, Voices from an Empire: A History of Afro-Portuguese Literature (Minneapolis: University of Minnesota Press, 1975), which not only surveys the literature but places it in its sociopolitical context.

II. GENERAL

Travel and Description

Almeida, F. J. M. de Lacerda e. Travessia de Africa.
Lisbon: Agência Geral das Colónias, 1936.

Andersson, Karl Johan. The Okavango River. London:
Harper, 1861.

Angelo of Gattina, Michael, and Denis de Carli of Piancen-
za. "A Curious and Exact Account of a Voyage to Congo
in the Years 1666 and 1667, " in A Collection of Voyages
and Travels, Vol. I. London: Awnsham Churchill, 1732,
pp. 554-558.

Arnot, F. S. Bihe and Garenganze or Four Years Further
Work and Travel in Central Africa. London: Hawkins,
1893.

_____. Garenganze: Or Seven Years Pioneer Mission
Work in Central Africa. London: Hawkins, 1889. (Reprint, Cass, 1969.)

Barbot, J. , and J. Casseneuve. "An Abstract of a Voyage
to the Congo River and to Cabinda in the Year 1700, " in
A Collection of Voyages and Travels, Vol. V, London:
Awnsham Churchill, 1732, pp. 497-522.

Barns, T. Alexander. Angolan Sketches. London: Methu-
en, 1928.

Bastian, A. Ein Besuch in San Salvador der Hauptstadt des
Königreichs Congo. Bremen: Strack, 1859.

_____. Die Deutsche Expedition an der Loango-Küste.
2 vols. Jena: Hermann Costenoble, 1874/1875.

Bateman, C. S. L. The First Ascent of the Kasai. London: Philip & Son, 1889.

Baum, H. Kunene-Sambesi Expedition. Berlin: Hermann Baum, 1903.

Baumann, H. Lunda: Bei Bauern and Jägern in Inner-Angola. Berlin: Würfel-Verlag, 1935.

Bentley, W. H. Pioneering on the Congo. 2 vols. London: Religious Tract Society, 1900. (Reprint, Johnson Reprint Corp., 1970).

Bowdich, Thomas. An Account of the Discoveries of the Portuguese in the Interior of Angola and Mozambique. London: J. Booth, 1824.

Burr, Malcolm. A Fossicker in Angola. London: Figurehead, 1933.

Burton, R. F. The Lands of Cazembe: Lacerda's Journey to Cazembe in 1798. London: J. Murray, 1873.

_____. Two Trips to Gorilla Land and the Cataracts of the Congo. 2 vols. London: Low, Marston and Searle, 1876.

Cameron, V. L. Across Africa. New York: Harper, 1877.

Capello, H., and R. Ivens. From Benguella to the Territory of Yacca. 2 vols. London: Sampson Low, 1882. (Reprint, Cass, 1969.)

Carvalho, H. A. Dias de. Expedição Portugueza ao Muatiamvu: Etnographia e História Tradicional dos Povos da Lunda. Lisbon: Imprensa Nacional, 1890.

_____. O Jagado de Cassange na Província de Angola. Lisbon: Typ. de C. A. Rodriques, 1898.

Cordoso, J. M. da Silva. No Congo Português, Viagem ao Bembe e Damba. Lisbon: Imprensa Nacional, 1913.

Crawford, Dan. Back to the Long Grass. London: Hodder and Stoughton, n. d.

_____. Thinking Black. London: Morgan and Scott, 1913.

Cuningham, Boyd. "A Pioneer Journey in Angola, " Geographical Journal, Vol. XXIV, July-December 1906, pp. 153-169.

Cushman, Mary Floyd. Missionary Doctor: The Story of Twenty Years in Africa. New York and London: Harper and Brothers, 1944.

Degrandpré, L. M. J. O'Hier. Voyage à la Côte Occidentale d'Afrique faits dans les Années 1786 et 1787. 2 vols. Paris: Librairie Dentu, 1801.

Faria, Francisco Leite de. Uma Relação de Rúi de Pina sobre o Congo escrita em 1492. Lisbon: Junta de Investigações Cientificas do Ultramar, 1966.

Freyberg, Hermann. Out of Africa. London: Hurst & Blackett, 1930.

Gibson, A. Between Cape Town and Loanda. London: W. Gardner, Darton & Co., 1905.

Graham, R. H. Carson. Under Seven Congo Kings: For Thirty-Seven Years a Missionary in Portuguese Congo. London: Carey Press, 1931.

Grenfell, W. David. The Dawn Breaks. London: Carey Press, 1948.

Harding, Colin. In Remotest Barotseland. London: Hurst and Blackett, 1904.

Huibregtse, Pieter Kornelis. Angola, the Real Story. The Hague: Forum, 1973.

Jaspert, F., and W. Jaspert. Through Unknown Africa: Experiences from the Jaspert African Expedition of 1926-1927. London: Jarrolds, 1929.

Jeannest, Charles. Quatre Années au Congo. Paris: G. Charpentier, 1884.

Johnston, H. H. The River Congo from Its Mouth to Bolobo. London: Sampson Low, 1884.

Lewis, T. These Seventy Years. London: Carey Press, 1930.

Livingstone, David.   Missionary Travels and Researches in South Africa.   London: J.   Murray, 1857.

Lux, Anton.   Von Loanda nach Kimbundu 1875-1876.   Vienna: Eduard Hölzel, 1880.

Magyard, Ladislaus (Laszlo).   Reisen in Süd-Afrika in den Jahren 1849 bis 1857.   Vol. I.   Pest-Leipzig, 1859. (New edition, Kraus, 1973.)

Mayo, The Earl of.   "A Journey from Mossamedes to the River Cunene, S. W. Africa," Proceedings of the Royal Geographical Society, n. s., Vol. V, No. 8, 1883, pp. 458-473.

Merolla, J.   "A Voyage to Congo and Several Other Countries Chiefly in Southern Africa," in A Collection of Voyages and Travels, Vol. I.   London: Awnsham Churchill, 1732, pp. 595-686.

Möller, P. A.   Journey in Africa Through Angola, Ovamboland and Damaraland [1899].   Cape Town: C. Struik, 1974.

Monteiro, J. J.   Angola and the River Congo.   2 vols. London: Macmillan, 1875.

Nascimento, J. P. do.   O Districto de Mossâmedes.   Lisbon: Typographia do Jornal 'As Colónias Portuguezas,' 1892.

Neto, J. P.   O baixo Cunene.   Lisbon: CEPS, 1963.

Neves, A. R.   Memória da Expedição a Cassange.   Lisbon: Imprensa Silviana, 1854.

Nitsche, G.   Ovamboland.   Kiel: C. Donath, 1913.

Omboni, Tito.   Viaggi nell'Africa Occidentale.   Milan: Civelli, 1846.

Owen, W. F. W.   Narrative of a Voyage to Discover the Shores of Africa, Arabia and Madagascar.   2 vols.   London: Richard Bentley, 1833.

Pereira, Pacheco.   Esmeraldo de Situ Orbis.   London: Hakluyt Society, 1936.

Pinto, A. A. da R. de Serpa. How I Crossed Africa. 2 vols. London: Bancroft, 1881.

Pinto, F. A. Angola e Congo. Lisbon: Livraria Ferreira, 1888.

Pogge, Paul. Im Reich des Muato-Yamwo. Berlin: D. Reimer, 1880.

Porto, A. F. da Silva. Silva Porto e a Travessia do Continente Africano. Lisbon: Agência Geral das Colónias, 1938.

_____. Viagens e Apontamentos de um Portuense em Africa. Lisbon: Agência Geral das Colónias, 1942.

Ravenstein, E. G. (ed.). The Strange Adventures of Andrew Battell of Leigh. London: Hakluyt Society, 1901.

Reade, W. W. Savage Africa. London: Smith, Elder & Co., 1864.

Sarmento, Alfredo de. Os Sertões d'Africa (Apontamentos de Viagem). Lisbon: F. A. da Silva, 1880.

Schachtzabel, A. Im Hochland von Angola. Dresden: Deutsche Buchwerkstätten, 1923.

Schütt, Otto H. Reisen im Südwestlichen Becken des Congo. Berlin: Dietrich Reimer, 1881.

Stanley, H. M. Through the Dark Continent, 1874-1877. London: Sampson, Low, Marston, Searle, 1878.

Statham, J. C. B. Through Angola--A Coming Colony. London: W. Blackwood & Sons, 1922.

Tams, George. Visit to the Portuguese Possessions in South-Western Africa. 2 vols. London: Newby, 1845. (Reprint, Negro Universities Press, 1969.)

Tuckey, J. K. Narrative of an Expedition to Explore the River Zaire. London: John Murray, 1818.

Valdez, F. Travrassos. Six Years of a Traveller's Life in Western Africa. 2 vols. London: Hurst and Blackett, 1861.

Vidal, J. E. de Lima. Por Terras d'Angola. Coimbra: F. Franco Amado, 1916.

Weeks, J. H. Among the Primitive Bakongo. London: Seeley, Service & Co., 1914.

Wentzel, V. "Angola, Unknown Africa," National Geographic, Vol. 120, 1961, pp. 347-383.

Interdisciplinary Works and General Information

Abshire, D. M., and M. A. Samuels (eds.). Portuguese Africa: A Handbook. New York: Praeger, 1969.

Africa Year Book and Who's Who 1977. London: Africa Journal Ltd., 1976.

"Angola," in Africa South of the Sahara, 1977-1978. London: Europa Publications, 1977, pp. 131-160. (Essays by René Pélissier and Basil Davidson.)

"Angola," in John Dickie and Alan Rake (eds.), Who's Who in Africa: The Political, Military and Business Leaders in Africa. London: Africa Development, 1973.

Chilcote, R. H. Portuguese Africa. Englewood Cliffs, N. J.: Prentice-Hall, 1967.

Duffy, James. "The Portuguese Territories," in C. Legum, et al. (eds.), Africa: Handbook for the Continent. 2d edition. New York: Praeger, 1965, pp. 283-302.

Fauvet, Paul. "Angola," in Richard Synge (ed.), Africa Guide 1978. London: Africa Guide Company, 1978, pp. 83-90.

Gonzaga, Noberto. Angola: A Brief Survey. Lisbon: Agência Geral do Ultramar, 1967.

Herrick, A. B., et al. Area Handbook for Angola. Washington, D. C.: American University Foreign Areas Studies Division, 1967.

Lefort, René. "Angola," in P. Biarnes, et al. L'Année Politique Africaine, 1976. Dakar: Société Africaine d'Edition, 1977, pp. 43-48.

Guides, Maps, Statistical Abstracts

Angola, Província de. Anuário Estatístico. Direcção dos
Serviços de Estatística (annual reports in the colonial
period; an ongoing source for data on such subjects as
population figures, education, trade, etc.).

Associação Industrial de Angola.   Guia Industrial de Angola.
Luanda: 1960.

Banco de Angola. Economic and Financial Survey.   (Annual
reports; also, Boletim Trimestral.)

Carta de Angola (1: 2, 000, 000).   3d edition.   Lisbon: Junta
de Investigações do Ultramar, 1973.

Gosseweiler, John, and F. A. Mendonça.   Carta Fitogeo-
gráfica de Angola.   Lisbon: Ministério das Colónias,
1939.

Lima, Mesquitela.   Carta Etnica de Angola.   Esbôço.   Luanda: IICA, 1970.

Mouta, Fernando.   Carta Geológica de Angola.   Lisbon:
Oficinas Gráficas da Imprensa do Anuário Comercial,
1933.

Portugal.   Anuário Estatístico do Ultramar (annual).

Redinha, José.   Carta Etnica da Província de Angola.   Luanda: CITA, 1966.

Bibliography, Guides to Archives, Historiography

Bender, Gerald J.   Portugal in Africa: A Bibliography of
the UCLA Collection.   Los Angeles: UCLA African
Studies Center, Occasional Papers, No. 12, 1972.

Bender, Gerald J. , and Allen Isaacman.   "The Changing
Historiography of Angola and Mozambique, " in C. Fyfe
(ed.), The Changing Direction of African Studies Since
1945.   A Tribute to Basil Davidson.   London: Longman,
1976, pp. 220-248.

Birmingham, David.   "Themes and Resources of Angolan
History, " African Affairs, Vol. 73, No. 291, 1974, pp.
188-203.

Borchert, Paul. Bibliographie de l'Angola 1500-1910. Brussels: Institut de Sociologie, 1912.

Brooks, George E. "Notes on Research Facilities in Lisbon and the Cape Verde Islands, " International Journal of African Historical Studies, Vol. VI, No. 2, 1973, pp. 304-314.

Chilcote, Ronald H. "African Ephemeral Materials: Portuguese African Nationalist Movements, " Africana Newsletter, Vol. I, Winter 1963, pp. 9-17.

_____. "Documenting Portuguese Africa, " Africana Newsletter, Vol. I, No. 3, 1963, pp. 16-36.

_____. Emerging Nationalism in Portuguese Africa: Vol. I: A Bibliography of Documentary Ephemera Through 1965. Stanford, Calif.: Hoover Institution Press, 1969 and 1972.

Conover, Helen F. A List of References on the Portuguese Colonies in Africa (Angola, Cape Verde Islands, Mozambique, Portuguese Guinea, São Thomé and Príncipe). Washington, D. C.: Library of Congress, Division of Bibliography, 1942.

El-Khawas, Mohamed A., and Francis A. Kornegay (eds.). American-Southern African Relations: Bibliographic Essays. Westport, Conn.: African Bibliography Center (New Series, No. 1), 1976.

Flores, Michel. "A Bibliographic Contribution to the Study of Portuguese Africa (1965-1972), " Current Bibliography on African Affairs, Vol. 7, No. 2, Spring 1976, pp. 116-137.

Gibson, Mary Jane. Portuguese Africa: A Guide to Official Publications. Washington, D. C.: Library of Congress, General Reference and Bibliography Division, Reference Department, 1967.

Gonçalves, José Júlio. Bibliografia Antropológica do Ultramar Português. Lisbon: Agência Geral do Ultramar, 1960.

_____. Bibliografia do Ultramar Português Existente na Sociedade de Geografia de Lisboa, Fasc. IV. Angola. Lisbon: 1963.

Greenwood, Margaret J. Angola: A Bibliography. Cape
   Town: University of Cape Town, School of Librarianship,
   1967.

Henderson, Robert d'A. "Portuguese Africa: Materials in
   English and in Translation, " Africa Research and Docu-
   mentation, No. 11 (1976), pp. 20-24, and No. 12 (1977),
   pp. 15-19.

Jadin, Louis. "L'Ancien Congo et les Archives de l'Oude
   West Indische Compagnie conservée à le Haye (1641-1648), "
   in Bulletin des Séances, Académie Royale des Sciences
   Coloniales, Vol. I, No. 3, 1955, pp. 447-451.

_____. "Importance des Acquisitions Nouvelles des Arch-
   ives Historique de l'Angola à Luanda pour l'Histoire de
   l'Afrique Centrale, 1726-1915, " Bulletin des Séances,
   Académie Royale des Sciences d'Outre-Mer, 1966, Pt. 6,
   pp. 892-1903.

_____. "Recherches dans les Archives et Bibliothèques
   d'Italie et du Portugal sur l'Ancien Congo, " Bulletin des
   Séances, Académie Royal des Sciences Coloniales, Vol.
   II, No. 6, 1956, pp. 951-990.

Miller, Joseph C. "Angola Before 1900--A Research Note, "
   African Studies Review, Vol. XX, No. 1, 1977, pp. 103-
   116.

_____. "The Archives of Luanda, Angola, " International
   Journal of African Historical Studies, Vol. VII, No. 4,
   1974, pp. 551-590.

Moser, Gerald. A Tentative Portuguese-African Bibliography:
   Portuguese Literature in Africa and African Literature in
   the Portuguese Language. University Park, Penn.: State
   Universities, Libraries Bibliographical Series, 3, 1970.

Pélissier, René. "Contribution à la Bibliographie de l'Angola
   (XIXe-XXe Siècles), " Genève-Afrique, Vol. XV, No. 2,
   1976, pp. 136-151.

_____. "Elements de Bibliographie: l'Afrique Portugaise
   dans les Publications de la Junta de Investigações do Ultramar (Lisbonne), " Genève-Afrique, Vol. IV, No. 2, 1965,
   pp. 249-270.

_____. "Etat de la Littérature Militaire relative à l'Afrique Australe Portugaise, " Revue française d'Etudes Politiques Africaines, No. 74, 1974, pp. 58-89.

Roteiro Topográfico dos Avulsos. Luanda: IICA, Arquivo Histórico de Angola, 1969.

Roteiro Topográfico dos Códices. Luanda: IICA, Arquivo Histórico de Angola, 1966.

Serrano, C. M. H. "Angola (1961-1976): Bibliografia, " Journal of Southern African Affairs, Vol. II, No. 3, July 1977, pp. 295-321.

Smaldone, Joseph P. African Liberation Movements: An Interim Bibliography. Waltham, Mass.: African Studies Association, Brandeis University, 1974.

Werner, Manfred W. Angola: A Selected Bibliography, 1960-1965. Washington, D.C.: Library of Congress, 1965.

Wheeler, Douglas. "Towards a History of Angola: Problems and Sources, " in Boston University Papers on Africa, Vol. IV, 1969, pp. 45-68.

Zubatsky, David S. A Guide to Resources in United States Libraries and Archives for the Study of Cape Verde, Guinea (Bissau), São Tomé-Príncipe, Angola and Mozambique. Durham, N.H.: Essays in Portuguese Studies, Essay No. 1, International Conference Group on Modern Portugal, mimeo, Spring 1977.

Periodicals and Newspapers: Portugal, Angola, Liberation Movements

Periodicals

Titles of the main English-language journals can be found in specific citations throughout this bibliography. The following is an indication of the main periodicals published in Portugal and Angola. The publication of several pre-1974 journals has now been suspended.

Periodicals: Portugal

Annaes do Conselho Ultramarino (Lisbon). 1854-64.

Annaes Marítimos e Colóniaes (Lisbon). 1840-46.

Arquivos das Colónias (Lisbon). 1917-33.

Boletim da Sociedade de Geografia de Lisboa (Lisbon). 1876- .

Boletim Geral do Ultramar (Lisbon). 1925-61. (Also known as Boletim da Agência Geral das Colónias; Boletim Geral das Colónias.)

Diário do Governo. 1715- . (The official Portuguese government gazette.) 1953- .

Portugal em Africa (Lisbon). 1894- . (A Catholic periodical.)

Studia (Lisbon, Centro de Estudos Históricos Ultramarinos). 1958-74.

Ultramar (Lisbon). (Journal of the Portuguese international community.) 1960-74.

Periodicals: Angola

Actividade Económica de Angola (Luanda). 1936-74.

Arquívos de Angola (Luanda). First Series: 1933-39; Second Series: 1943- .

Boletim Cultural (Museu de Angola). 1960- .

Boletim da Associação Industrial de Angola (Luanda). 1949-74.

Boletim do Instituto de Angola (Luanda). 1953-74.

Boletim Oficial do Governo Geral da Província de Angola (Luanda). 1845-1975. (Official gazette.)

Instituto de Investigação Científica de Angola (Luanda): Boletim. 1962- . Memórias e Trabalhos. 1960- .

Mensário Administrativo (Luanda).

Publicações Culturais da Companhia de Diamantes de Angola (Diamang; Serviços Culturais, Museu do Dundo). 1946-74.

Trabalho (Luanda). 1960-74.

Liberation-Movement Publications

The bibliography by Joseph Smaldone, African Liberation Movements: An Interim Bibliography (Waltham, Mass.: African Studies Association, 1974), contains some information on publications issued by the liberation movements. Some of the periodicals, such as Kwacha-Angola (UNITA, London), Angola in Arms (MPLA, Dar es Salaam), and Angola: Bulletin d'Information (Léopoldville/Kinshasa, FNLA), are available on microfilm from the Cooperative Africana Microforms Project (CAMP, 5721, Cottage Avenue, Chicago, IL 60637).

Newspapers

It is difficult to keep track of the many newspapers that have flourished and declined in Angola in the past century or so, but they are potentially a prime source of historical information. A great expansion in popular journalism in the late nineteenth century was part of the growing expression of African nationalism. The articles of Douglas Wheeler, for example (1970 and 1972), cite some of these publications. The following is a guide to some of the others. As of 1978 the Journal de Angola (formerly the Província de Angola) is the only Luanda daily newspaper.

Feuereisen, Fritz, and Ernst Schmake (comps.). "Angola, " in Africa: A Guide to Newspapers and Magazines. New York: Africana Publishing Corporation, 1969, pp. 21-25.

Kitchen, Helen. "Portuguese Africa, " in Helen Kitchen (ed.), The Press in Africa. Washington, D. C.: Ruth Sloan Associates, 1956, pp. 92-96.

Lopo, Júlio de Castro. Jornalismo de Angola: Subsídios para a sua História. Luanda: Centro de Informação e Turismo de Angola, 1964.

_____ . "Subsídios para a História do Jornalismo de Angola," in Arquívos de Angola, Vol. VIII, Nos. 31-36, 1951, pp. 91-114.

III.   HISTORICAL

General

Andrade, Mário Pinto de.   "Qu'est-ce que le 'luso-tropical-ism'?"   Présence Africaine, No. 4, October-November 1955, pp. 24-35.

Anonymous.   "Notes sur Cabinda, Partie Intégrante de l'Angola, " Revue Française d'Etudes Politiques Africaines, No. 121, January 1976, pp. 58-69.

Axelson, Eric.   Congo to Cape, Early Portuguese Explorers. London: Faber and Faber, 1973.

Axelson, Sigbert.   Culture Confrontation on the Lower Congo. (Studia Missionalia Upsaliensa XIV.)   Stockholm: Gummerson, 1970.

Bastide, Roger.   "Lusotropicology, Race, and Nationalism, and Class Protest and Development in Brazil and Portuguese Africa, " in Ronald H. Chilcote (ed.), Protest and Resistance in Angola and Brazil.   Berkeley: University of California Press, 1972, pp. 225-242.

Bender, Gerald J.   Angola Under the Portuguese: The Myth and the Reality.   Berkeley: University of California Press, 1978.

Birmingham, David.   "Central Africa from Cameroun to the Zambezi, " in Richard Gray (ed.), Cambridge History of Africa, Vol. IV.   New York: Cambridge University Press, 1975, pp. 325-383.

_____.   "Central Africa from Cameroun to the Zambezi, " in Roland Oliver (ed.), Cambridge History of Africa, Vol. III.   New York: Cambridge University Press, 1977, pp. 519-566.

_____. "The Forest and the Savanna of Central Africa, "
in John E. Flint (ed.), Cambridge History of Africa, Vol.
V. New York: Cambridge University Press, 1976, pp.
222-269.

_____. "Portuguese Rule in Angola, " Tarikh, Vol. IV,
No. 4, 1976, pp. 25-36.

Boavida, A. Angola: Five Centuries of Portuguese Exploitation. Richmond, Canada: Liberation Support Movement,
1972.

Boxer, C. R. Four Centuries of Portuguese Expansion,
1415-1823: A Succinct Survey. Johannesburg: Witwatersrand University Press, 1961.

_____. The Portuguese Seaborne Empire, 1415-1825.
London: Hutchinson, 1969.

_____. Race Relations in the Portuguese Colonial Empire,
1415-1825. Oxford: Clarendon Press, 1963.

Brásio, António. Angola. Spiritana Monumenta Histórica.
Séries Africanas, 5 vols. Pittsburgh: Duquesne University Press, 1970.

_____. História e Missionologia: Inéditos e Esparsos.
Luanda: IICA, 1973.

_____. Monumenta Missionária Africana: Africa Oci-
dental. First Series, 11 vols. Lisbon: Agência Geral
do Ultramar, 1952-71. Second Series: 4 vols. Lisbon:
1958- .

Chilcote, Ronald H. (ed.). Protest and Resistance in Angola
and Brazil: Comparative Studies. Berkeley: University
of California Press, 1972.

Childs, G. M. "The Chronology of the Ovimbundu Kingdoms, " Journal of African History, Vol. XI, No. 2, 1970,
pp. 241-248.

_____. "The Kingdom of Wambu (Huambo): A Tentative
Chronology, " Journal of African History, Vol. V, No. 3,
1964, pp. 367-379.

Cordeiro, Luciano. Questões Histórico-Colóniais.   3 vols.
Lisbon: Ministério das Colónias, 1935-36.

_____. Viagens, Explorações e Conquistas dos Portu-
gueses: Colleção de Documentos. 6 vols. Lisbon: Imprensa Nacional, 1881.

Davidson, Basil. The African Awakening. London: Cape,
1955.

Delgado, Ralph. Ao Sul do Cuanza: Ocupação e Aproveita-
mento do Antigo Reino de Benguela, 1483-1942. 2 vols.
Lisbon: Imprensa Beleza, 1944.

_____. História de Angola. 4 vols. Benguela and Lob-
ito: Edição da Tip. do Jornal de Benguela, 1948-55.

Dias, G. Sousa. Os Portugueses em Angola. Lisbon:
Agência Geral do Ultramar, 1959.

Duffy, James. Portugal in Africa. Baltimore: Penguin,
1962.

_____. Portuguese Africa. Cambridge: Harvard Univer-
sity Press, 1959.

Felgas, H. A. E. História do Congo Português. Carmona:
Emprêsa Gráfica do Uige, 1958.

Felner, A. de A. Angola: Apontamentos Sobre a Colonização dos Planaltos e Litoral do Sul de Angola. Documentos. 3 vols. Lisbon: Agência Geral das Colónias,
1940.

Franque, Domingos José. Nós, Os Cabindas. Lisbon: Editôra Argo, 1940.

Freitas, Amadeu José de. Angola: O Longo Caminho da
Liberdade. Lisbon: Moraes Editores, 1975.

Freyre, Gilberto. The Portuguese and the Tropics. Lisbon:
Gráfica Santelmo, 1961.

Gann, L. H., and P. Duignan. White Settlers in Tropical
Africa. Baltimore: Penguin, 1962.

Gibson, Gordon D. "Himba Epochs," History in Africa, Vol.
IV, 1977, pp. 67-122.

Godinho, Vitorino de Magalhães. Documentos sobre a Ex-
pansão Portuguesa. Lisbon: Editorial Gleba, 1943-56.

_____. L'Economie de l'Empire Portugais aux XVe et XVIe Siècles. Paris: SEVPEN, 1969.

Gray, Richard, and David Birmingham (eds.). Pre-Colonial African Trade: Essays on Trade in Central and Eastern Africa before 1900. London: Oxford University Press, 1970.

Hammond, Richard J. "Economic Imperialism: Sidelights on a Stereotype, " Journal of Economic History, Vol. XXI, No. 4, December 1961, pp. 582-598.

_____. "Uneconomic Imperialism: Portugal in Africa Before 1910, " in L. H. Gann and P. Duignan (eds.), Colonialism in Africa, 1870-1960, Vol. I. New York: Cambridge University Press, 1969, pp. 352-382.

Henriksen, Thomas H. "Portugal in Africa: A Non-Economic Interpretation, " African Studies Review, Vol. XVI, No. 3, December 1973, pp. 405-416.

Katzenellenbogen, Simon. Railways and the Copper Mines of Katanga. Oxford: Clarendon Press, 1973.

Kimambo, Isaria. "The Rise of the Congolese State Systems, " in T. O. Ranger (ed.), Aspects of Central African History, London: Heinemann, 1968, pp. 29-48.

Lemos, Alberto de. História de Angola. Lisbon: R. da Oliveira, 1932.

Lima, J. J. Lopes de. Ensaios sobre a Statística das Possessões Portuguezas na África Occidental e Oriental, Vol. III: Angola e Benguella. Lisbon: Imprensa Nacional, 1846.

MacGaffey, Wyatt. "Oral Tradition in Central Africa, " International Journal of African Historical Studies, Vol. VII, No. 3, 1975, pp. 417-426.

_____. "The West in Congolese Experience, " in P. Curtin (ed.), Africa and the West. Madison: University of Wisconsin Press, 1972, pp. 49-74.

Martin, Phyllis M. "The Cabinda Connection: An Historical Perspective, " African Affairs, Vol. 76, No. 302, January 1977, pp. 47-59.

Martins, Joaquim. Cabindas: História, Crença, Usos e Costumes. Cabinda: Comissão de Turismo da Câmara Municipal de Cabinda, 1972.

Mattos, R. J. da Cunha. Compêndio Histórico das Possessões de Portugal na Africa. Rio de Janeiro: Ministério da Justiça e Negócios Interiores, 1963.

Mauro, F. Le Portugal et l'Atlantique au XVIIe Siècle, 1570-1670. Paris: SEVPEN, 1960.

Milheiros, Mário. Indice Histórico--Corográfico de Angola. Luanda: IICA, 1972.

Miller, Joseph C. Equatorial Africa. Washington, D. C.: American Historical Association, 1976.

_____. "Kings, Lists and History in Kasanje, " History in Africa, Vol. 6, 1979, pp. 51-96.

Mota, A. Teixeira da. A Cartografia Antiga da Africa Central e a Travessia entre Angola e Moçambique, 1500-1860. Lourenço Marques: Sociedade de Estudos de Moçambique, 1964.

MPLA, Centro de Estudos Angolanos. História de Angola. Porto: Edições Afrontamento, 1975.

Oliveira, Mário António F. de, and Carlos A. M. do Couto. Angolana (Documentação Sobre Angola), Vol. I, 1783-1883; Vol. II, 1883-1887. Luanda: IICA, 1968 and 1971.

Palmer, Robin, and Neil Parsons (eds.). The Roots of Rural Poverty in Central and Southern Africa. London: Heinemann, 1977.

Pélissier, René. "Angola: La Guerre de Cent Ans?" Etudes, Vol. 348, No. 2, February 1978, pp. 149-166.

Rego, António da Silva. "Portugal and Africa: A Historical Survey, 1482-1961, " in C. P. Potholm and R. Dale (eds.), Southern Africa in Perspective: Essays in Regional Politics. New York: Free Press, 1972, pp. 157-171.

Rodney, Walter. "European Activity and African Reaction in Angola, " in T. O. Ranger (ed.), Aspects of Central African History. London: Heinemann, 1968, pp. 49-70.

Rodrigues, J. H.   Brazil and Africa.   Berkeley: University
of California Press, 1965.

_____.   "The Influence of Africa on Brazil and of Brazil
on Africa, " Journal of African History, Vol. III, No. 1,
1962, pp. 49-67.

Thornton, John.   "The State in African Historiography: A
Reassessment, " Ufahamu (UCLA), Vol. IV, No. 2, 1973,
pp. 113-126.

Vansina, Jan.   "The Bells of Kings, " Journal of African
History, Vol. X, No. 2, 1969, pp. 187-198.

_____.   Kingdoms of the Savanna.   Madison: University
of Wisconsin Press, 1966.

_____.   "Long Distance Trade Routes in Central Africa, "
Journal of African History, Vol. III, No. 3, 1962, pp.
375-390.

Wheeler, Douglas L.   "A Note on Smallpox in Angola, 1670-
1875, " Studia, Vol. XIII-XIV, January-July 1964 , pp. 351-
362.

_____.   "Rebels and Rebellions in Angola, 1672-1892, " in
Mark Karp (ed.), African Dimensions: Essays in Honor
of William O. Brown.   Boston: Boston University African
Studies Center, 1975, pp. 81-93.

_____, and René Pélissier.   Angola.   New York: Praeg-
er, 1971.   (Reprint, Greenwood Press, 1978.)

Early History to the Late Eighteenth Century

Abreu e Brito, Domingos de.   Um Inquérito à Vida Adminis-
trativa e Econômica de Angola e do Brasil em Fins do
Século XVI.   Coimbra: Imprensa da Universidade, 1931.

Bal, Willy.   Le Royaume du Congo aux XVe et XVIe Siècles.
Léopoldville: Editions de l'Institut National d'Etudes Politiques, 1963.

_____ (ed.).   Description du Royaumme de Congo et des
Contrées Environnnantes, par Filippo Pigafetta et Duarte
Lopes (1591).   Louvain: Nauwelaerts, 1963.

Balandier, Georges. Daily Life in the Kingdom of the Kongo from the Sixteenth to the Eighteenth Century. London: George Allen and Unwin, 1968.

Birmingham, David. "The African Response to Early Portuguese Activities in Angola, " in Ronald H. Chilcote (ed.), Protest and Resistance in Angola and Brazil. Berkeley: University of California Press, 1972, pp. 11-28.

_____. "The Date and Significance of the Imbangala Invasion of Angola, " Journal of African History, Vol. VI, No. 2, 1965, pp. 143-152.

_____. "Early African Trade in Angola and Its Hinterland, " in R. Gray and D. Birmingham (eds.), Pre-Colonial African Trade. London: Oxford University Press, 1970, pp. 163-174.

_____. The Portuguese Conquest of Angola. London: Oxford University Press, Institute of Race Relations, 1965.

_____. Trade and Conflict in Angola: The Mbundu and Their Neighbours Under the Influence of the Portuguese, 1483-1790. Oxford: Clarendon Press, 1966.

Bontinck, François. Brève Relation de la Fondation de la Mission des Frères Mineurs Capucins ... au Royaume de Congo. Louvain: Nauwelaerts, 1964.

_____. Diaire Congolais de Fra Luca da Caltanisetta, 1690-1701. Louvain: Nauwelaerts, 1970.

_____. "Histoire du Royaume du Congo (c. 1624), " Etudes d'Histoires Africaine, Vol. IV, 1972, pp. 5-145.

_____. Jean-François de Rome. La Fondation de la Mission des Capucins au Royaume de Congo (1648). Louvain: Nauwelaerts, 1964.

_____. "Notes complementaires sur Dom Nicolau Agau Rosada e Sardonia, " African Historical Studies, Vol. II, No. 1, 1968, pp. 101-119.

Boxer, C. R. "Background to Angola: Cadornega's Chronicle, " History Today, Vol. XI, 1961, pp. 665-672.

_____. "The Old Kingdom of Congo, " in Roland Oliver

(ed.), The Dawn of African History. London: Oxford
University Press, 1961, pp. 75-81.

_____. Portuguese Society in the Tropics: The Munici-
pal Councils of Goa, Macao, Bahia and Luanda, 1580-1800.
Madison: University of Wisconsin Press, 1965.

_____. "Salvador Correia de Sá e Benavides and the Re-
conquest in 1648, " Hispanic American Historical Review,
Vol. XXVIII, 1948, pp. 483-513.

_____. Salvador de Sá and the Struggle for Brazil and
Angola, 1602-1686. London: University of London, 1952.

Cadornega, António de Oliveira. História Geral das Guerras
Angolanas, 1681. Revised and annotated by Manuel Alves
da Cunha. 3 vols. Lisbon: Agência Geral das Colónias,
1940-42.

Cardoso, J. C. Feo. Memórias Contendo, a História dos
Governadores e Capitaens Generaes de Angola. Paris:
Fantin, 1825.

Cavazzi de Montecuccolo, P. João António. Istórica De-
scrizione de'tre Regni, Congo. Matamba e Angola.
Bologna: G. Monti, 1687 (French translation: see
Labat (1732); German translation: 1694; Portuguese
translation: 1965).

Childs, G. M. "The Peoples of Angola in the Seventeenth
Century According to Cadornega, " Journal of African History, Vol. I, No. 2, 1960, pp. 271-279.

Correa, Elias Alexandre da Silva. História de Angola
(eighteenth century). 2 vols. Lisbon: Agência Geral
das Colónias, 1937.

Couto, Carlos A. M. do. O Zimbo na Históriografia Angolana. Luanda: IICA, 1973.

_____. Os Capitães-Mores em Angola no Século XVIII.
Luanda: IICA, 1972.

Cuvelier, J. L'Ancien Royaume de Congo. Brussels:
Desclée de Brouwer, 1946.

_____. Documents sur une Mission Française au Kakongo,

1766-1776. Brussels: Mémo., Institut Royal Colonial
Belge, 1953.

_____. Relations sur le Congo du Père Laurent de
Lucques, 1700-1797. Brussels: Mémo., Institut Royal
Colonial Belge, 1953.

_____, and L. Jadin. L'Ancien Congo d'après les Arch-
ives Romaines, 1514-1640. Brussels: Mémo., Académie
Royale des Sciences Coloniales, 1954.

Dapper, Olfert. Naukeurige Beschrijvinge des Afrikaensche
Gewesten. 2d edition. Amsterdam: Jacob van Meurs,
1676.

Dias, G. Sousa. Pioneiros de Angola: Explorações Portuguesas do Sul de Angola. Lisbon: Agência Geral das
Colónias, 1937.

Duysters, L. "Histoire des Aluunda, " Problèmes d'Afrique
Centrale, Vol. XII, No. 40, 1958, pp. 75-81.

Felner, A. de A. Angola: Apontamentos Sôbre a Ocupação
e Início do Estabelecimento dos Portugueses no Congo.
Coimbra: Imprensa da Universidade, 1933.

Haveaux, G. La Tradition Historique des Bapende Orientaux.
Brussels: Mémo., Institut Royal Colonial Belge, 1954.

Heintze, Beatrix. "Historical Notes on the Kisama of Angola, " Journal of African History, Vol. XIII, No. 3, 1972,
pp. 407-418.

_____. "Unbekanntes Angola: Der Staat Ndongo im 16
Jahrhundert, " Anthropos, Vol. 72, 1977, pp. 749-805.

Herbert, Eugenia W. "Portuguese Adaptation to Trade Patterns, Guinea to Angola (1443-1640), " African Studies Review, Vol. 2, September 1974, pp. 411-423.

Jadin, Louis. "Le Congo et la Secte des Antoniens. Rest-
auration du Royaume sous Pedro IV et la 'Saint-Antoine'
Congolaise (1694-1718), " Bulletin de l'Institut Historique
Belge de Rome, Vol. XXXIII, 1961, pp. 411-615.

_____. "Relations sur le Royaume du Congo du P. Dai-
mondo de Dicomano, Missionnaire de 1791 à 1798, "

Bulletin de l'Académie Royale des Sciences Coloniales, Vol. XXXIII, 1961, pp. 411-615.

_____. "Rivalités Luso-Néerlandaises au Sohio, Congo, 1600-1675, " Bulletin de l'Institut Historique Belge de Rome, Vol. XXXVII, 1966, pp. 137-351.

Labat, J. B. Relation Historique de l'Ethiopie Occidentale. 5 vols. Paris: Delespine, 1732.

Manso, Paiva. História do Congo (Documentos) 1492-1772. Lisbon: Typ. de Academia, 1877.

Martin, Phyllis. The External Trade of the Loango Coast, 1576-1870: The Effects of Changing Commercial Relations on the Vili Kingdom of Loango. Oxford: Clarendon Press, 1972.

_____. "The Trade of Loango in the 17th and 18th Centuries, " in R. Gray and D. Birmingham (eds.), Pre-Colonial African Trade. London: Oxford University Press, 1970, pp. 139-161.

Miller, Joseph C. "The Imbangala and the Chronology of Early Central African History, " Journal of African History, Vol. XIII, No. 4, 1972, pp. 549-574.

_____. Kings and Kinsmen: Early Mbundu States in Angola. Oxford: Clarendon Press, 1976.

_____. "A Note on Kasanze and the Portuguese, " Canadian Journal of African Studies, Vol. VI, 1972, pp. 43-56.

_____. "Nzinga of Matamba in a New Perspective, " Journal of African History, Vol. XVI, No. 2, 1975, pp. 201-216.

_____. "Requiem for the 'Jaga, ' " Cahiers d'Etudes Africaines, Vol. XIII, 1 (No. 49), 1973, pp. 121-149.

Proyart, L. B. Histoire de Loango, Kakongo et Autres Royaumes d'Afrique. Paris: Berton and Crapart, 1776.

Randles, W. G. L. L'Ancien Royaume du Congo, des Origines à la Fin du XIXe Siècle. Paris: Mouton, 1968.

Rego, António da Silva. O Ultramar Português no Século XVIII. Lisbon: Agência Geral do Ultramar, 1967.

Thornton, John. "Demography and History in the Kingdom of Kongo, 1550-1750, " Journal of African History, Vol. XVIII, No. 4, 1977, pp. 507-530.

_____. "New Light on Cavazzi's Seventeenth Century Description of Kongo, " History in Africa, Vol. 6, 1979, pp. 253-264.

Vansina, Jan. "The Foundation of the Kingdom of Kasanje, " Journal of African History, Vol. IV, No. 3, 1963, pp. 355-374.

_____. "More on the Invasions of Kongo and Angola by the Jaga and the Lunda, " Journal of African History, Vol. VII, No. 3, 1966, pp. 421-429.

_____. "Notes sur l'Origine du Royaume de Kongo, " Journal of African History, Vol. IV, No. 1, 1963, pp. 33-38.

Vellut, Jean-Luc. "Notes sur le Lunda et la Frontière Luso-Africaine, (1700-1900), " Etudes d'Histoire Africaine, Vol. III, 1972, pp. 61-166.

_____. "Relations Internationales du Moyen-Kwango et de l'Angola dans la Deuxieme Moitié du XVIIIe Siècle, " Etudes d'Histoire Africaine, Vol. I, 1970, pp. 75-135.

_____. "Le royaume de Cassange et les Réseaux Luso-Africains (ca. 1750-1810), " Cahiers d'Etudes Africaines, Vol. XV, 1 (No. 57), 1975, pp. 117-136.

Wilson, Anne. "The Kongo Kingdom to the Mid-Seventeenth Century, " unpublished Ph. D. thesis. London University, 1978.

Nineteenth and Twentieth Centuries

Almeida, João de. Sul d'Angola: Relatório de um Governo de Distrito (1908-1910). 2d ed. Lisbon: Agência Geral das Colónias, 1936.

Anstey, Roger T. Britain and the Congo in the Nineteenth Century. Oxford: Clarendon Press, 1962.

Axelson, Eric. Portugal and the Scramble for Africa, 1875-

123 Bibliography

1891.   Johannesburg: Witwatersrand University Press,
1967.

Bailey,   Norman A.   "Local and Community Power in Angola, " Western Political Quarterly, Vol. 21, September
1968, pp. 400-408.

Bandeira,   Sá de.   Facts and Statements Concerning the Right
of the Crown of Portugal to the Territories of Molembo,
Cabinda, Ambriz, and Other Places on the West Coast of
Africa.   London: Fitch, 1877.

Birmingham,   David.   "The Coffee Barons of Cazengo, "
Journal of African History, Vol. XIX, No. 4, 1978, pp.
523-538.

Brásio,   António (ed.).   Dom António Barroso, Missionário,
Cientista, Missiólogo.   Lisbon: Centro de Estudos Históricos Ultramarinos, 1961.

Broadhead,   Susan Herlin.   "Trade and Politics on the Congo
Coast, 1770-1870, " unpublished Ph. D. thesis.   Boston
University, 1971.

Carvalho e Menezes,   J. A. de.   Memória Geográfica e
Política das Possessões Portuguesas n'Affrica Occidental.
Lisbon: Typografia Carvalhense, 1834.

Chagas,   M. J. Pinheiro.   As Colónias Portuguezas no Século XIX, 1811-1890.   Lisbon: A. M. Pereira, 1890.

Clarence-Smith,   W. G.   "Capitalist Penetration Among the
Nyaneka of Southern Angola, 1760s to 1920s, " African
Studies, Vol. 37, No. 2, 1978, pp. 163-176.

_____.   Mossamedes and Its Hinterland, 1875-1915,
unpublished Ph. D. thesis.   London University,
1975.

_____.   "The Myth of Uneconomic Imperialism: The
Portuguese in Angola 1836-1926, " Journal of Southern African Studies, Vol. 5, No. 2, 1979, pp. 165-180.

_____.   "The Thirstland Trekkers in Angola: Some Re-
flections on a Frontier Society, " The Societies of Southern
Africa in the 19th and 20th Centuries.   Collected Seminar
Papers, University of London Institute of Commonwealth
Studies, Vol. VI, 1976, pp. 42-51.

_____, and R. Moorsom. "Underdevelopment and Class Formation in Ovamboland, 1845-1915, " Journal of African History, Vol. XVI, No. 3, 1975, pp. 365-382. (Also published as a chapter in Palmer and Parsons, 1977, pp. 96-112.)

Cordeiro, Luciano. Portugal and the Congo: A Statement. London: E. Stanford, 1883.

Couceiro, Henrique Mitchell de Paiva. Angola. Dois Anos de Governo. Junho de 1907-Junho de 1909. 2d edition. Lisbon: Editora A. Nacional, 1948.

Dias, Jill R. "Black Chiefs, White Traders and Colonial Policy near the Kwanza: Kabuku Kambilo and the Portuguese, 1873-1896, " Journal of African History, Vol. XVII, No. 2, 1976, pp. 276-290.

Dias, Manuel da Costa. Colonização dos Planaltos de Angola. Lisbon: Tipografia Mendongração Nacional, 1913.

Drechsler, Horst. "Germany and South Angola, 1898-1903, " Présence Africaine, Vol. 14/15, 1962, pp. 51-69.

Eça, António Pereira de. A Campanha do Sul de Angola em 1915. Lisbon: Imprensa Nacional, 1923.

Egerton, F. C. C. Angola in Perspective. London: Routledge and Kegan Paul, 1957.

_____. Angola Without Prejudice. Lisbon: Agência Geral do Ultramar, 1955.

Esterhuyse, J. South-West Angola, 1880-1884. Cape Town: C. Struik, 1968.

Galvão, Henrique. Angola: Para uma Nova Política. Vol. I: Fisionomia do Passado, Aspectos do Presente. Lisbon: Livraria Popular de F. Franco, 1937.

Hammond, Richard J. Portugal and Africa, 1815-1910. A Study in Uneconomic Imperialism. Stanford, Calif.: Stanford University Press, 1966.

_____. "Race Attitudes and Policies in Portuguese Africa in the 19th and 20th Centuries, " Race, Vol. 9, No. 2, October 1967, pp. 205-216.

_____. "Some Economic Aspects of Portuguese Africa in the Nineteenth and Twentieth Centuries, " in P. Duignan and L. H. Gann (eds.), Colonialism in Africa, 1870-1960 (IV: The Economics of Colonialism). Cambridge: Cambridge University Press, 1975, pp. 250-280.

Machado, Ernesto. No Sul de Angola. Lisbon: Agência Geral do Ultramar, 1956.

Mattos, J. d'Almeida. O Congo Português e As Suas Riquezas. Lisbon: Simões, 1924.

Mayo, Earl of. De Rebus Africanus. The Claims of Portugal to the Congo and Adjacent Littoral, with Remarks on the French Annexation. London: W. H. Allen and Co., 1883.

Miller, Joseph C. Cokwe Expansion, 1850-1900. Madison: University of Wisconsin, African Studies Committee, Occasional Papers, No. 1, 1969. Second revised printing, 1974.

_____. "Cokwe Trade and Conquest, " in Richard Gray and David Birmingham (eds.), Pre-Colonial African Trade. London: Oxford University Press, 1970, pp. 175-201.

Nascimento, J. Pereira do. A Colonisação de Angola. Lisbon: Typografia Mendonça, 1912.

Norton de Matos, J. M. R. A Província de Angola. Porto: Edição de Maranus, 1926.

_____. A Situação Financeira e Económica da Província de Angola. Lisbon: Tipografia da Cooperativa Militar, 1914.

Pélissier, René. "Campagnes Militaires au Sud-Angola, 1885-1915, " Cahiers d'Etudes Africaines, Vol. IX, No. 33, 1969, pp. 54-123.

_____. La Colonie du Minotaure: Nationalismes et Révoltes en Angola, (1926-1961). Montamets, France: Pélissier, 1978.

_____. Les Guerres Grises: Résistance et Révoltes en Angola (1845-1941). Montamets, France: Pélissier, 1977.

_____. "Mandume et un Resistance Ovambo au Colonial-isme Portugais en Angola, " in C.-A. Julien, et al. (eds.), Les Africains. Editions Jeunes Afriques: Vol. VIII, 1978, pp. 205-257.

Pinto, F. Latour da Veiga. Le Portugal et Le Congo au XIXe Siècle. Paris: Presses Universitaires de France, 1972.

Pinto, Júlio Ferreira. Angola: Notas e Comentários de um Colôno. Lisbon: Instituto Superior de Comércio de Lisboa, 1926.

Rebelo, M. da Silva. Relações entre Angola e Brasil, 1808-1830. Lisbon: Agência Geral do Ultramar, 1970.

Rego, António da Silva. O Ultramar Português no Século XIX. Lisbon: Agência Geral do Ultramar, 1966.

Roçadas, José Augusto, Alves. Relatório sobre as Opera-ções no Sul de Angola em 1914. Lisbon: Imprensa Nacional, 1919.

Santos, Eduardo dos. A Questão da Lunda, 1885-1894. Lisbon: Agência Geral do Ultramar, 1966.

Soremekun, Fola. "The Bailundu Revolt in Angola in 1902, " African Social Research, Vol. 16, December 1973, pp. 447-471.

_____. "Trade and Dependency in Central Angola: The Ovimbundu in the Nineteenth Century, " in Robin Palmer and Neil Parsons (eds.), The Roots of Rural Poverty in Central and Southern Africa. London: Heinemann, 1977, pp. 82-95.

Stamm, Anne. "La Société Créole à Saint-Paul de Loanda dans les Années 1836-1848, " Revue Française d'Histoire d'Outre Mer, Vol. 59, No. 217, June 1977, pp. 578-610.

Tabler, Edward C. Pioneers of South West Africa and Ngamiland, 1738-1880. Cape Town: A. A. Balkema, 1973.

Wheeler, Douglas L. "African Elements in Portugal's Armies in Africa, 1961-1974, " Armed Forces and Society, Vol. II, No. 2, February 1976, pp. 233-250.

_____. "Angola Is Whose House? Early Stirrings of An-
golan Nationalism and Protest, 1822-1910, " International
Journal of African Historical Studies, Vol. II, No. 1,
1969, pp. 1-23.

_____. "An Early Angolan Protest: The Radical Jour-
nalism of José Fontes Pereira (1823-1891), " in Robert I.
Rotberg and Ali A. Mazrui (eds.), Protest and Power in
Black Africa. New York: Oxford University Press, 1970,
pp. 854-874.

_____. "Livingstone and Angola: Some New Letters,
1854-1856, " Rhodes-Livingstone Journal, Vol. XXXII, December 1962, pp. 23-45.

_____. "Nineteenth Century African Protest in Angola:
Prince Nicolas of Kongo (1830?-1860), " African Historical
Studies, Vol. I, No. 1, 1968, pp. 40-59.

_____. "Origins of African Nationalism in Angola: As-
similado Protest Writings, 1859-1929, " in Ronald H. Chilcote (ed.), Protest and Resistance in Angola and Brazil.
Berkeley and Los Angeles: University of California Press,
1972, pp. 67-87.

_____. "Portugal in Angola: A Living Colonialism?" in
C. P. Potholm and R. Dale (eds.), Southern African in
Perspective: Essays in Regional Politics. New York:
Free Press, 1972, pp. 172-182.

_____. "The Portuguese Army in Angola, " Journal of
Modern African Studies, Vol. VII, No. 3, October 1969,
pp. 425-439.

_____. Portuguese Expansion in Angola Since 1836: A
Re-Examination. (Central African Historical Association
Pamphlet No. 20.) Salisbury: 1967.

_____, and C. Diane Christensen. "To Rise With One
Mind: The Bailundo War of 1902, " in Franz-Wilhelm
Heimer (ed.), Social Change in Angola. Munich: Welt-
forum Verlag, 1973, pp. 53-92.

Slavery, Slave Trade, and Forced Labor

Anstey, Roger T. The Atlantic Slave Trade and British

Abolition, 1760-1810. Atlantic Highlands, N. J.: Humanities Press, 1975.

————. "The Volume and Profitability of the British Slave Trade, 1761-1807, " in Stanley L. Engermann and Eugene D. Genovese (eds.), Race and Slavery in the Western Hemisphere: Quantitative Studies. Princeton: Princeton University Press, 1975, pp. 3-32.

Baião, R. J. "Brief Glimpses of Labor Questions in the Portuguese Province of Angola, " Trabalho, No. 5, 1964, pp. 85-101.

Bailey, Norman A. "Native and Labor Policy, " in D. M. Abshire and M. A. Samuels, Portuguese Africa: A Handbook. New York: Praeger, 1969, pp. 165-177.

Bethell, L. The Abolition of the Brazilian Slave Trade: Britain, Brazil and the Slave Trade Question, 1807-1869. Cambridge: Cambridge University Press, 1970.

Birmingham, David. "Central Africa and the Atlantic Slave Trade, " in Roland Oliver (ed.), The Middle Age of African History. London: Oxford University Press, 1967, pp. 56-62.

Bouët-Willaumez, L. E. Commerce et Traite des Noirs aux Côtes Occidentales d'Afrique. Paris: Imprimérie Nationale, 1848.

Bourne, H. R. Fox. Slave Traffic in Portuguese Africa: An Account of Slave-Trading in Angola and of Slavery in the Islands of San Thome and Principe. London: P. S. King & Son, 1908.

Cadbury, William A. Labour in Portuguese West Africa. London: George Routledge, 1910. (Reprint Negro Universities Press, 1969.)

Clarence-Smith, W. G. "Slavery in Coastal Southern Angola, 1875-1913, " Journal of Southern African Studies, Vol. II, No. 2, April 1976, pp. 214-223.

Cunha, J. M. da Silva. O Trabalho Indígena. 2d edition. Lisbon: Agência Geral do Ultramar, 1955.

Curtin, Philip D. The Atlantic Slave Trade: A Census. Madison: University of Wisconsin Press, 1969.

Davidson, Basil. "Africa's Modern Slavery, " Harper's, 209 (1250), 1956, pp. 56-63.

_____. Black Mother. London: Gollancz, 1961. (Published in the U.S. as The African Slave Trade: Precolonial History, 1450-1850. Boston: Little, Brown, 1961.)

Duffy, James. A Question of Slavery: Labour Policies in Portuguese Africa and the British Protest, 1850-1920. Oxford: Clarendon Press, 1967.

Durieux, André. Essai sur le Statut des Indigènes de la Guinée, de l'Angola et du Mozambique. Brussels: Mémo., Académie Royale des Sciences Coloniales, 1955.

Harris, John H. Portuguese Slavery: Britain's Dilemma. London: Methuen, 1913.

International Labor Organization. Report of the Commission to Examine the Complaint Filed by the Government of Ghana Concerning the Observance by the Government of Portugal of the Abolition of Forced Labor Convention 1957. Geneva: 1962.

Keith, Henry. "Masters and Slaves in Portuguese Africa in the 19th Century: First Soundings, " Studia, Vol. 33, December, 1971, pp. 235-249.

Klein, Herbert S. The Middle Passage: Comparative Studies in the Atlantic Slave Trade. Princeton: Princeton University Press, 1978.

_____. "The Portuguese Slave Trade from Angola in the 18th Century, " Journal of Economic History, Vol. XXXII, No. 4, 1972, pp. 894-918.

_____. "The Trade in African Slaves to Rio de Janeiro, 1795-1811, " Journal of African History, Vol. X, No. 4, 1969, pp. 533-549.

_____, and Stanley L. Engerman. "Shipping Patterns and Mortality in the Slave Trade to Rio de Janeiro, 1825-1830, " Cahiers d'Etudes Africaines, Vol. XV, No. 3, 1975, pp. 381-398.

Labour: Forced or Free? London: Committee for Freedom in Mozambique, Angola and Guinea, Topics No. 1, n. d.

MacGaffey, Wyatt. "Economic and Social Dimensions of
   Kongo Slavery, " in S. Miers and I. Kopytoff (eds.),
   Slavery in Africa: Historical and Anthropological Perspectives. Madison: University of Wisconsin Press,
   1977, pp. 235-257.

Miller, Joseph C. "Imbangala Lineage Slavery, " in S. Miers and I. Kopytoff (eds.), Slavery in Africa: Historical
   and Anthropological Perspectives. Madison: University
   of Wisconsin Press, 1977, pp. 205-233.

_____. "Legal Portuguese Slaving from Angola. Some
   Preliminary Indications of Volume and Direction, 1760-
   1830, " Revue Française d'Histoire d'Outre-Mer, Vol.
   Vol. LXII, Nos. 226-227, 1975, pp. 135-176.

_____. "The Slave Trade in Congo and Angola, " in
   Martin L. Kilson and Robert I. Rothberg (eds.), The
   African Diaspora: Interpretive Essays. Cambridge:
   Harvard University Press, 1976, pp. 75-113.

_____. "Slaves, Slavers and Social Change in Nineteenth
   Century Kasanje, " in F. W. Heimer (ed.), Social Change
   in Angola. Munich: Weltforum Verlag, 1973, pp. 9-29.

Nevinson, Henry Wood. A Modern Slavery. New York:
   Harper, 1906. (Reprint, Metro Books, 1972.)

_____. More Change, More Chances. London: Nisbet,
   1925.

Perrings, Charles. Black Mineworkers in Central Africa.
   London: Heinemann, 1979.

_____. "Good Lawyers but Poor Workers: Recruited
   Angolan Labour in the Copper Mines of Katanga, 1917-
   1921, " Journal of African History, Vol. XVIII, No. 2,
   1977, pp. 237-259.

Roçadas, José Augusto Alves. La Main d'Oeuvre Indigène à
   Angola. Lisbon: Imp. 'A Editora Limitada', 1914.

Slavery in Portuguese Africa: Opposing Views (containing
   works by Nevinson and Monteiro). (Reprint, Metro Books,
   1972.)

IV. POLITICAL

Nationalism and Guerrilla Warfare

Addicott, Len. Cry Angola! London: SCM Press, 1962.

Andrade, Mário de. "Angolese Nationalism, " Présence Africaine, No. 42/43, 1962 (English Edition Vol. 14/15), pp. 7-23.

_____. Liberté pour l'Angola. Paris: François Maspero, 1962.

_____, and Marc Ollivier. The War in Angola: A Socio-Economic Study. Dar es Salaam: Tanzanian Publishing House, 1976.

Angola: A Symposium; Views of a Revolt. London: Oxford University Press, Institute of Race Relations, 1962.

"Angola Casebook, " Présence Africaine, Vol. XVII, No. 45, 1963, pp. 151-196.

Barnett, Don (ed.). Liberation Support Movement Interview: Daniel Chipenda. Richmond, B. C. : Liberation Support Movement Information Center, 1972.

_____. The Making of a Middle Cadre: Rui de Pinto. (Life Histories from the Revolution: Angola, MPLA No. 1.) Richmond, B. C. : Liberation Support Movement Information Center, 1973.

_____, and Roy Harvey (eds.). With the Guerrillas in Angola. Richmond, B. C. : Liberation Support Movement Information Center, 1970.

_____. The Revolution in Angola: MPLA Life Histories and Documents. Indianapolis: Bobbs-Merrill, 1972.

Bender, Gerald J. "Angola: History, Insurgency and Social Change, " Africa Today, Vol. 19, No. 1, Winter 1972, pp. 30-36.

_____. "The Limits of Counterinsurgency: An African Case, " Comparative Politics, Vol. 4, April 1972, pp. 331-360.

César, Amândio. Angola 1961. Lisbon: Verbo, 1961.

Chilcote, Ronald H. Emerging Nationalism in Portuguese Africa: Vol. II. Documents. Stanford, Calif.: Hoover Institution Press, 1972.

Davezies, R. Les Angolais. Paris: Editions de Minuit, 1965.

_____. La Guerre d'Angola. Bordeaux: Ducros, 1968.

Davidson, Basil. "Angola in the Tenth Year: A Report and an Analysis, May-July 1970, " in African Affairs, Vol. 70, No. 278, 1971, pp. 37-49.

_____. In the Eye of the Storm: Angola's People. Garden City, N.Y.: Doubleday, 1972.

_____. "An Inside Look at Angola's Fight for Freedom, " Africa Report, Vol. 15, December 1970, pp. 16-18.

_____. "The Liberation Struggle in Angola and 'Portuguese' Guinea, " African Quarterly, Vol. 10, No. 1, 1970-71, pp. 25-39.

_____. Walking 300 Miles with Guerrillas Through the Bush of Eastern Angola. Pasadena: California Institute of Technology, Munger Africana Library Notes, No. 6, April 1971.

Davis, John A., and James K. Baker (eds.). Southern Africa in Transition. New York: Praeger, 1966.

Duffy, James. Portugal's African Territories: Present Realities. New York: Carnegie Endowment for International Peace, Occasional Papers No. 1., 1962.

Ehnmark, Anders, and Per Wästberg. Angola and Mozambique: The Case Against Portugal. London: Pall Mall Press, 1963.

Felgas, Hélio A. E. Guerra em Angola. Lisbon: Livraria Clássica, Editora A. M. Texeira, 1961.

Ferreira, E. de Sousa. Portuguese Colonialism in Africa: The End of an Era. Paris: UNESCO, 1974.

First, Ruth. Portugal's Wars in Africa. London: International Defence and Aid Fund for Southern Africa, 1971.

Gibson, Richard. African Liberation Movements: Contemporary Struggles Against White Minority Rule. London: Oxford University Press, Institute of Race Relations, 1972.

Gilchrist, Sidney. Angola Awake. Toronto: Ryerson Press, 1968.

Grundy, Kenneth W. Confrontation and Accommodation in Southern Africa. Berkeley and Los Angeles: University of California Press, 1973.

_____. Guerrilla Struggle in Africa. New York: Grossman Publishers, 1971.

Houser, G. M. "Nationalist Organizations in Angola: Status of the Revolt, " in J. A. Davis and J. K. Baker (eds.), Southern Africa in Transition. New York: Praeger, 1966, pp. 157-179.

Humbaraci, Arslan, and Nicole Muchnik. Portugal's African Wars: Angola, Guinea-Bissau, Mozambique. London: Macmillan, 1974.

Jack, Homer. Angola: Repression and Revolt in Portuguese Africa. New York: American Committee on Africa, 1960.

Kagombe, Maina D. "African Nationalism and Guerrilla Warfare in Angola and Mozambique, " in C. P. Poltholm and R. Dale (eds.), Southern Africa in Perspective: Essays in Regional Politics. New York: Free Press, 1972, pp. 196-205.

Legum, Colin. "Guerrilla Warfare and African Liberation Movements, " Africa Today, Vol. 14, No. 4, August 1967, pp. 5-10.

Lemarchand, René. "The Bases of Nationalism Among the Bakongo, " Africa, Vol. XXXI, October 1961, pp. 344-354.

Liberation in Southern Africa: The Organization of Angolan
Women.   Chicago Committee for the Liberation of Angola,
Mozambique and Guinea, (1476 W. Irving Park Road,
Chicago, IL 60613), 1976.

Marcum, John.   "The Angola Rebellion: Status Report, "
Africa Report, February 1964, pp. 3-7.

_____.   The Angolan Revolution, Vol. I: The Anatomy of
an Explosion, 1950-1962.   Cambridge: MIT Press, 1969.

_____.   The Angolan Revolution, Vol. II: Exile Politics
and Guerrilla Warfare, 1962-1976.   Cambridge: MIT
Press, 1978.

_____.   "The Exile Condition and Revolutionary Effective-
ness: South African Liberation Movements, " in C. P.
Potholm and R. Dale (eds.), Southern Africa in Perspective, New York: Free Press, 1972, pp. 262-275.

_____.   "Three Revolutions: Angola, Mozambique and
Portuguese Guinea, " Africa Report, Vol. XII, November
1967, pp. 9-22.

MPLA.   Revolution in Angola.   London: Merlin Press, 1972.

Neto, Agostinho.   Messages to Companions in the Struggle,
Speeches by Agostinho Neto.   Richmond, B. C. :   Liberation
Support Movement Information Center, 1972.

_____.   "Who Is the Enemy?   What Is Our Objective? "
Ufahamu (UCLA), Vol. IV, No. 3, 1974, pp. 109-120.

Panikkar, Kavalam M.   Angola in Flames.   London: Asian
Publishing House, 1962.

Parsons, Clifford J.   "Background to the Angola Crisis, "
The World Today, Vol. XVII, July 1961, pp. 278-288.

Pélissier, René.   "Nationalismes en Angola, " Revue Française de Science Politique, Vol. 19, 1969, pp. 1187-1215.

_____.   "Origines du Mouvement Nationaliste Moderniste
en Angola, " Revue Française d'Etudes Politiques Africaines, 126, 1976, pp. 14-47.

Poltholm, Christian P. , and Richard Dale.   Southern Africa
in Perspective.   New York: Free Press, 1972.

Rivers, Bernard. "Angola: Massacre and Oppression, "
Africa Today, Vol. 21, Winter 1974, pp. 41-45.

Samuels, Michael A. "The Nationalist Parties, " in D. M.
Abshire and M. A. Samuels (eds.), Portuguese Africa:
A Handbook. New York: Praeger, 1969, pp. 389-405.

Santos, Eduardo dos. Maza: Elementos de Etno-História
para a Interpretação do Terrorismo no Noreste de Angola.
Lisbon: Edição do Autor, 1965.

Teixeira, Bernardo. The Fabric of Terror: Three Days in
Angola. New York: Devin-Adair Company, 1965.

Valahu, Mugur. Angola, Cléf de l'Afrique. Paris: Nouvelles Editions Latines, 1966.

Venter, Al. The Terror Fighters: A Profile of Guerrilla
Warfare in Southern Africa. Cape Town: Purnell, 1969.

_____. Portugal's Guerrilla War: The Campaign for Af-
rica. Cape Town: J. Malherbe, 1973.

Waring, Ronald. The War in Angola, 1961. Lisbon: Tip.
Silvas, 1962.

Wästberg, Olle. Angola. Stockholm: Bokforlaget PAN/
Norstedts, 1970.

Wheeler, Douglas L. "Reflections on Angola, " Africa Report, Vol. 12, November 1967, pp. 58-62.

Whitaker, Paul M. "The Revolutions of 'Portuguese Africa, ' " Journal of Modern African Studies, Vol. VIII, No.
1, 1970, pp. 15-35.

Women of the Revolution. London: Committee for Freedom
in Mozambique, Angola, and Guinea, Topics No. 3, n. d.

Politics Since 1974

Adelman, Kenneth. "Report from Angola, " Foreign Affairs,
Vol. 53, April 1975, pp. 558-574.

Angola After Independence: Struggle for Supremacy. London:
Institute for the Study of Conflict, No. 64, 1975.

"Angola: Can UNITA Survive?" Africa Confidential, Vol. 20, No. 4, August 14, 1979, pp. 1-3.

"Angola: Neto's Troubles, " Africa Confidential, Vol. 19, No. 2, 1978, pp. 1-4.

"Angola: Puzzling Both East and West, " Africa Confidential, Vol. 20, No. 2, January 17, 1979, pp. 1-3.

"Angola: The UNITA Thorn, " Africa Confidential, Vol. 20, No. 11, May 23, 1979, pp. 1-2.

Angola: The Independence Agreement. Lisbon: Ministry of Mass Communication, 1975.

"Angola: Unita Renews Its Challenge, " Africa Confidential, Vol. 18, No. 17, August 19, 1977, pp. 3-4.

Angola: 11 de Novembro de 1975 Documentos de Independência (Documents de l'Independence; Documents of Independence). Ediçăo do Ministério da Informaçăo. Luanda: Imprensa Nacional, 1975.

Barratt, J. The Angolan Conflict. Braamfontein: South African Institute of International Affairs, 1976.

Birmingham, David. "The Twenty-Seventh of May: An Historical Note on the Abortive 1977 Coup in Angola, " African Affairs, Vol. 77, No. 309, October 1978, pp. 554-564.

Brown, Kevin. "Report from Luanda: A New Angolan Society, " The Nation, July 17-24, 1976, pp. 42-46.

Carreira, António. Angola: da escravatura ao trabalho livre. Lisbon: Arcádia, 1977.

Clington, Mário de Souza. Angola Libre? Paris: Gallimard, 1975.

"The Constitution of MPLA into a Party of the Working Class, " People's Power (London), No. 11, January-March 1978, pp. 38-49.

Cosse, J. P. , and J. Sanchez. Angola: Le Prix de la Liberté. Paris: Syros, 1976.

Cruz, V. Pompílio da. Angola: Os Vivos e os Mortes. Lisbon: Editorial Intervenção, 1976.

Dash, Leon. Savimbi's 1977 Campaign Against the Cubans and MPLA-Observed for 7½ Months, and Covering 2100 Miles Inside Angola. Pasadena: California Institute of Technology, Munger Africana Library Notes, No. 40/41, December 1977.

Davidson, Basil. "Angola: A Success that Changes History, " Race and Class, Vol. 18, No. 1, 1976, pp. 23-37.

_____. "Bandits and Invaders, " West Africa, July 25, 1977, pp. 1518-1521.

_____. "Questions of Nationalism, " African Affairs, Vol. 76, No. 302, 1977, pp. 39-46.

_____. "Towards a New Angola, " People's Power (London), No. 9, 1977, pp. 1-5.

Davis, Jennifer, George N. Houser, Susan Rogers, and Herb Shore. No One Can Stop The Rain: Angola and the MPLA. New York: The Africa Fund, 1976.

Gjerstad, Øle. The People in Power: An Account from Angola's Second War of National Liberation. Oakland: LSM Information Center, 1976.

Groupe Afrique Centrale du Cedetim. Angola: La Lutte Continue. Paris: François Maspero, 1977.

Heimer, Franz-Wilhelm. "Décolonisation et Legitimité Politique en Angola, " La Revue Française d'Etudes Politiques Africaines, Vol. 126, June 1976, pp. 48-72.

_____. "Les Dilemmes de la Décolonisation en Angola, " Cultures et Developpement, Vol. VIII, No. 1, 1976, pp. 3-42.

Henriksen, Thomas H. "People's War in Angola, Mozambique and Guinea-Bissau, " Journal of Modern African Studies, Vol. XIV, No. 3, 1976, pp. 377-399.

Hodges, Tony. "Angola" in Colin Legum (ed.), Africa Contemporary Record, Vol. 7, 1974-1975. New York: Africana Publishing Corporation, 1975, pp. B527-B545.

_____. "Angola, " in Colin Legum (ed.), Africa Contempo-
rary Record, Vol. 8, 1975-1976. New York: Africana
Publishing Corporation, 1976.

_____. "Angola, " in Colin Legum (ed.), Africa Contempo-
rary Record, Vol. 9, 1976-1977. New York: Africana
Publishing Corporation, 1977, pp. B445-B461.

Lecoff, George. Angola, l'Indépendance Empoisonnée.
Paris: Presses de la Cité, 1976.

Marcum, John. "Angola: Division or Unity?" in Gwendolen
M. Carter and Patrick O'Meara (eds.), Southern Africa
in Crisis. Bloomington: Indiana University Press, 1977,
pp. 136-162.

_____. "Angola: Perilous Transition to Independence, "
in Gwendolen M. Carter and Patrick O'Meara (eds.),
Southern Africa: The Continuing Crisis. Bloomington:
Indiana University Press, 1979, pp. 175-198.

_____. "The Anguish of Angola: On Becoming Indepen-
dent in the Last Quarter of the Twentieth Century, " Issue
(ASA, Waltham, Mass.), Vol. V, No. 4, Winter 1975,
pp. 3-12.

_____, Gerald Bender and Douglas Wheeler. "Testimony
on Angola--June 16, 1975, " Issue, Vol. V, No. 3, 1975,
pp. 16-23.

MPLA. Angola: A Tentativa de Golpe de Estado de 27
Maio de 77. Lisbon: 1977.

MPLA. Road to Liberation: MPLA Documents on the Founding of the People's Republic of Angola. Oakland: LSM
Information Center, August 1976 (first printing); February
1977 (second printing).

MPLA: "The Story of the First Congress, " People's Power,
(London) No. 11, (January-March 1978), pp. 33-37.

People's Press Angola Book Project. With Freedom in Their
Eyes: A Photo-Essay of Angola, 1976. San Francisco:
People's Press, 1976.

Pereira, Sá. Angola em Chamas. Lisbon: Literal, 1977.

Santos, Fernando Barciela. Angola na Hora Dramática da
Descolonização. Lisbon: Prêlo, 1975.

Sousa, Valdemiro de. Angola: A Guerra e o Crime. 2d
edition. Planeta: Editorial Formação, 1976.

Foreign Affairs

Foreign Affairs: Portugal and
Portuguese-Speaking Africa

Bender, Gerald. "Portugal and Her Colonies Join the Twentieth Century: Causes and Initial Implications of the Military Coup, " Ufahamu (UCLA), Vol. 4, No. 3, Winter
1974, pp. 150-155.

Bruce, Neil. Portugal: The Last Empire. New York:
Wiley, 1975.

Caetano, Marcello. Relações das Colónias de Angola e
Moçambique com os Territórios Estrangeiros Vizinhos.
Lisbon: Imprensa Nacional de Lisboa, 1946.

Figueiredo, António de. Portugal and Its Empire. London:
Gollancz, 1961.

_____. Portugal. Fifty Years of Dictatorship. New
York: Holmes & Meier, 1976.

Gann, L. H. "Portugal, Africa and the Future, " Journal of
Modern African Studies, Vol. XIII, March 1975, pp. 1-18.

Henriksen, Thomas H. "End of an Empire: Portugal's Collapse in Africa, " Current History, Vol. 68, No. 405,
1975, pp. 211-215.

_____. "Mozambique and Angola: Revolution and Inter-
vention, " Current History, November 1976, pp. 153-157.

_____. "Portugal's Changing Fortunes in Africa, " Cur-
rent History, March 1973, pp. 106-110, 130-131.

Kay, Hugh. Salazar and Modern Portugal. London: Eyre
& Spottiswoode, 1970.

Miller, Joseph C. "The Politics of Decolonization in Portuguese Africa, " African Affairs, Vol. 72, No. 295, 1975, pp. 135-147.

Minter, William. Portuguese Africa and the West. Baltimore: Penguin, 1972.

Saul, J. S. "The Revolution in Portugal's African Colonies, " Canadian Journal of African Studies, Vol. 9, No. 2, 1975, pp. 315-336.

Smith, Alan K. "António Salazar and the Reversal of Portuguese Colonial Policy, " Journal of African History, Vol. XV, No. 4, 1974, pp. 653-667.

Sykes, John. Portugal and Africa: The People and the War. London: Hutchinson, 1971.

Foreign Affairs: Southern Africa

Africa Research Group (Boston). Race to Power: The Struggle for Southern Africa. Garden City, N. Y.: Doubleday, 1974.

"Angola: South Africa Hesitates, " Africa Confidential, Vol. 17, No. 6, March 19, 1976, pp. 6-7.

Carter, Gwendolen M. , and Patrick O'Meara (eds.). Southern Africa in Crisis. Bloomington: Indiana University Press, 1977.

_____. Southern Africa: The Continuing Crisis. Bloomington: Indiana University Press, 1979.

Davidson, Basil, Joe Slovo, and Antony Wilkinson. Southern Africa: The New Politics of Revolution. Harmondsworth, Middlesex: Penguin, 1976.

Hallett, Robin. "The South African Intervention in Angola, " African Affairs, Vol. 77, No. 303, July 1978, pp. 347-386.

Legum, Colin. "The International Dimension of the Crisis in Southern Africa, " in Gwendolen M. Carter and Patrick O'Meara (eds.), Southern Africa in Crisis. Bloomington: Indiana University Press, 1977, pp. 3-14.

_____ . "The Soviet Union, China and the West in Southern Africa, " Foreign Affairs, Vol. 54, No. 4, 1976, pp.
745-762.

_____ , and Tony Hodges. After Angola: The War over
Southern Africa. London: Rex Collings, 1976.

Marcum, John. "Southern Africa After the Collapse of Por-
tuguese Rule, " in Helen Kitchen (ed.), Africa: From
Mystery to Maze. Lexington and Toronto: Lexington
Books, 1976, pp. 77-133.

Winston, John. "Réflexions sur l'Intervention Sud-Africaine
en Angola, " Revue Française d'Etudes Politiques Africaines, No. 142, October 1977, pp. 60-69.

Foreign Affairs: Rest of the World

"Angola: Diplomatic Jigsaw, " Africa Confidential, Vol. 19,
No. 14, 1978, pp. 1-3.

Azevedo, Mário J.   "Zambia, Zaire and the Angolan Crisis
Reconsidered, " Journal of Southern African Affairs, Vol.
II, No. 3, July 1977, pp. 274-294.

Baynham, S. J.   "International Politics and the Angolan
Civil War, " Army Quarterly and Defense Journal, January 1977, pp. 25-32.

Bender, Gerald J.   "Angola, the Cubans and American Anxi-
eties, " Foreign Policy, No. 31, Summer 1978, pp. 3-30.

_____ . "La Diplomatie de M. Kissinger et l'Angola, "
Revue Française d'Etudes Politiques Africaines, Vol. 126,
June 1976, pp. 73-95.

_____ . "Kissinger in Angola: Anatomy of Failure, " in
René Lemarchand (ed.), American Policy in Southern Af-
rica: The Stakes and the Stance. Washington, D. C. :
University Press of America, 1978, pp. 65-143.

Carvalho, J. M. Os Cubanos e. ... Lisbon: Livraria Popular de Francisco Franco, 1976.

Cervenka, Zdenek. "Cuba and Africa, " in Colin Legum (ed.),
Africa Contemporary Record, Vol. 9, 1976-1977. New
York: Africana Publishing Corporation, 1977, pp. A84-A90.

"Congo-B: Radicalisation and Angola, " Africa Confidential, Vol. 17, No. 2, January 23, 1976, pp. 3-6.

Davis, Nathaniel. "The Angola Decision in 1975: A Personal Memoir, " Foreign Affairs, Vol. 57, No. 1, Fall 1978, pp. 109-124.

Ebinger, Charles K. "External Intervention in Internal War: The Politics and Diplomacy of the Angolan Civil War, " Orbis, Vol. 20, No. 3, Fall 1976.

El-Khawas, Mohamed A. "American Involvement in Portuguese Africa: The Legacy of the Nixon Years, " Ufahamu (UCLA), Vol. VI, No. 1, 1975, pp. 117-130.

_____. "Power Struggle in Angola: Whose Struggle? Whose Power?" Journal of Southern African Affairs, Vol. I, Special Issue, October 1976, pp. 53-68.

Farber, Stephen B. "Gulf and Angola, " Issue, Vol. II, No. 3, Fall 1972, pp. 21-30.

Harsh, Ernest, and Tony Thomas (eds.). Angola, The Hidden History of Washington's Wars. New York: Pathfinder Press, 1976.

Hodges, Tony. "The Struggle for Angola: How the World Powers Entered a War in Africa, " The Round Table, Vol. 262, 1976, pp. 173-189.

Kissinger, C. Clark. "China and Angola, " Monthly Review, Vol. 28, No. 1, May 1976, pp. 1-17.

Larrabee, Stephen. "Moscow, Angola and the Dialectics of Détente, " World Today, Vol. 32, No. 5, May 1976, pp. 173-182.

Legum, Colin. "Foreign Intervention in Angola, " in C. Legum (ed.), Africa Contemporary Record, Vol. 8, 1975-1976. New York: Africana Publishing Corporation, 1976, pp. A3-A38.

Lipson, Charles. "Angola and the Memory of Vietnam, " The Nation, April 17, 1976, pp. 458-460.

Livingstone, Neil C., and Manfred Von Nordheim. "The United States Congress and the Angola Crisis, " Strategic Review, Vol. V, Spring 1977, pp. 34-44.

Marcum, John. "Lessons of Angola, " Foreign Affairs, Vol.
54, No. 3, April 1976, pp. 407-425.

_____. The Politics of Indifference: Portugal and Afri-
ca, a Case Study in American Foreign Policy. Syracuse,
N. Y.: Syracuse University, Eastern African Studies,
1972.

_____. "The U. S. and Portuguese Africa: A Perspective
on American Foreign Policy, " Africa Today, Vol. 18, No.
4, October 1971, pp. 23-37.

Margarido, Alfredo. "L'O. U. A. et les Territoires Portugais, " Revue Français d'Etudes Politiques Africaines,
No. 22, October 1967, pp. 82-106.

Minter, William. Imperial Network and External Dependency: The Case of Angola. Beverly Hills, Calif.: Sage
Publications, 1972.

_____. "Imperial Network and External Dependency: Im-
plications for the Angolan Liberation Struggle, " Africa
Today, Vol. 21, No. 1, 1974, pp. 25-39.

Morris, Roger. "The Proxy War in Angola: Pathology of
a Blunder, " New Republic January 31, 1976, pp. 19-23.

Partners in Crime: the Anglo-Portuguese Alliance Past and
Present. London: Committee for Freedom in Mozambique, Angola and Guinea, 1973.

Sibeko, Alexander. "The Battle for Angola, " African Communist, Vol. 62, 1975, pp. 41-51.

"Speaking Out on Angola, " Africa Report, Vol. 21, No. 1,
January-February 1976, pp. 2-17.

Stevens, Christopher. "The Soviet Union and Angola, " African Affairs, Vol. 75, No. 299, April 1976, pp. 137-146.

Stockwell, John. In Search of Enemies: A CIA Story. New
York: W. W. Norton, 1978.

United Nations. Report of the Subcommittee on the Situation
in Angola. S/4993 (November 22, 1961).

_____. Report of the Special Committee on Territories

under Portuguese Administration.   A7623/Add 3 (September 25, 1969).   General Assembly,   24th Session.

_____ .   Reports on Situation in Angola:
1970   Document A/AC. 109/L. 625/Add. 1,   May 8.
1970   Document A/8023/Add. 3,   October 5.
1971   Document SCI/71/4, July 14.
1971   Document A/8398/Add. 1, December 6.
1972   Document A/8723/Add. 3, September 1.
1973   Document A/AC. 109/L. 865, May 9.
1973   Document A/9023 (Part III), October 11.
1974   Document A/AC. 109/L 918, February 4.
1975   Document A/10023/Add. 1, November 20.

"U. N. Debate on Angola, " Présence Africaine, Vol. XIV-XV,
No. 42-43, 1962, pp. 85-164.

U. S. Congress.   House.   Committee on International Relations (U. S. Policy on Angola), III.   Washington, D. C. :
Government Printing Office, 1976.

_____ . _____ . _____ . Subcommittee on Africa.
Gerald Bender and John Stockwell, United States-Angolan Relations, May 25, 1978, pp. 1-39.

_____ .   Senate.   Committee on Foreign Relations.   Subcommittee on African Affairs.   Hearings on Angola ("U. S. Involvement in Civil War in Angola"), Washington, D. C. , 1976.

Wallerstein, Immanuel.   "Luanda Is Madrid, " The Nation,
Vol. 10, January 1976, pp. 12-17.

V. ECONOMIC

Abshire, David M. "Minerals, Manufacturing, Power and Communications, " in D. M. Abshire and M. A. Samuels, Portuguese Africa: A Handbook. New York: Praeger, 1969, pp. 294-319.

"Angola: Benguela--The Problem Railway, " African Confidential, Vol. 17, No. 19, September 24, 1976, pp. 1-4.

Angola: Ministério da Economia. Programa Económico de Angola. Luanda: 1975.

Anon. (R. B. B.). "Labor in Angola, " in Rural Africana, Vol. 24, 1974, pp. 75-88.

Araújo, A. Correia de. Aspectos do Desenvolvimento Económico e Social de Angola. Lisbon: Junta de Investigações do Ultramar, 1964.

Azevedo, J. M. Cerqueira de. Angola, Exemplo de Trabalho. Luanda: Edição do autor, 1958.

_____. Subsídios para o Estudo da Económico de Angola nos Últimos Cem Anos. Lisbon: Imprensa Nacional, 1965.

Botting, Douglas. "Triumph of the Benguela Railway, " Geographical Magazine, August 1967, pp. 255-269.

Brandenburg, Frank. "Development, Finance and Trade, " in D. M. Abshire and M. A. Samuels (eds.), Portuguese Africa: A Handbook. London: Praeger, 1969, pp. 219-252.

_____. "Transport Systems and Their External Ramifications, " in D. M. Abshire and M. A. Samuels, Portuguese Africa: A Handbook. New York: Praeger, 1969, pp. 320-344.

Carneiro, Carlos. O Mar de Angola. Luanda: Imprensa
Gráfica de Angola, 1949.

Castro, E. G. de Albuquerque e. Angola: Portos e Trans-
portes. Luanda: Ofícinas Gráficas, ABC, 1974.

Committee for Freedom in Mozambique, Angola and Guiné.
White Power: The Cunene River Scheme. London: 1973.

Companhia do Caminho de Ferro de Benguela. Benguela
Railway. Benguela: 1960.

Companhia de Diamantes de Angola. A Short Report on Its
Work in Angola. Lisbon: Diamang, 1963.

"Cunene Scheme May Attract More Guerrillas Than Settlers, "
African Development, July 1972, pp. 14-16.

Diogo Júnior, Alberto. Rumo à Industrialização de Angola.
Luanda: Neográfica Limitada, 1963.

Galvão, H. Informação Económica sobre Angola. Lisbon:
1932.

Guerra, Henrique Lopes. Angola: Estrutura Económica e
Classes Sociais. Luanda: Livrangol, 1975.

Hammond, Richard J. Portugal's African Problems: Some
Economic Facets. New York: Carnegie Endowment for
Peace, 1962.

Hance, W. A. , and I. S. Van Dongen. "The Port of Lobito
and the Benguela Railway, " Geographical Review, Vol.
XLVI, No. 4, October 1956, pp. 460-487.

Houk, Richard J. "Prospects and Problems of Petroleum
Production in Angola, " Tijdschrift voor Economische en
Sociale Geografie, Vol. 49, 1958, pp. 105-191.

_____. "Recent Development in the Portuguese Congo, "
Geographical Review, Vol. XLVIII, April 1958, pp. 201-
221.

Leeming, F. A. "An Estimate of the Domestic Output of
Angola and Mozambique, " South African Journal of Economics, Vol. XXVIII, June 1960, pp. 141-154.

Léfèbvre, Gabriel. L'Angola: Son Histoire, Son Economie.
Liège: Thone, 1947.

Marques, Walter. Problemas do Desenvolvimento Económico
de Angola. 2 vols. Luanda: Junta de Desenvolvimento
Industrial, 1964.

Mendes, Afonso. O Trabalho Assalariado em Angola. Lisbon: Instituto Superior de Ciências Sociais e Política
Ultramarina, 1966.

Miracle, Marvin P. Maize in Tropical Africa. Madison:
University of Wisconsin Press, 1966.

Niddrie, David L. "The Cunene River: Angola's River of
Life, " Journal of the American Portuguese Cultural Society, Vol. 6, Winter-Spring 1970, pp. 1-17.

_____. "The Role of Ground Transport in the Economic
Development of Angola, " Journal of the American Portuguese Cultural Society, Vol. 3, Winter-Spring 1969, pp.
1-13.

Recenseamento Agrícola de Angola. 27 vols. Luanda: Missão de Inquéritos Agricolas de Angola, 1963-72.

Santos, A. C. V. Thomaz dos. Perspectivas Económicas de
Angola. Lisbon: Agência Geral das Colónias, 1949.

Santos, Augusto L. Ferreira dos. Estructura do Comércio
Externo de Angola: Alguns Aspectos. Lisbon: Junta de
Investigações do Ultramar, 1959.

Sharman, T. C. Portuguese West Africa: Economic and
Commercial Conditions in Portuguese West Africa (Angola).
London: Overseas Economic Surveys, 1954.

Steiner, Herbert H. Angola's Agricultural Economy in Brief.
Foreign Agricultural Economic Report No. 139. Washington, D. C. : U. S. Department of Agriculture Economic Research Service, 1977.

Van Dongen, Irene S. "Agriculture and Other Primary Production, " in D. M. Abshire and M. A. Samuels, Portuguese Africa: A Handbook. New York: Praeger, 1969,
pp. 253-293.

_____. "Coffee Trade, Coffee Regions and Coffee Ports of Angola, " Economic Geography, Vol. XXXVII, No. 4, October 1961, pp. 320-346.

_____. "The Port of Luanda in the Economy of Angola, " Boletim da Sociedade de Geografia de Lisboa, Series 78a, No. 1-3, January-March 1960, pp. 3-42.

_____. "Sea Fisheries and Fish Ports in Angola, " Boletim da Sociedade de Geografia de Lisboa, January-March 1962, pp. 3-30.

_____. "La Vie Economique et les Ports de l'Enclave de Cabinda (Angola), " Cahiers d'Outre-Mer (Bordeaux), Vol. XV, 1962, pp. 5-24.

Varian, H. F.   Some African Milestones.   Oxford: G. Ronald, 1953.

Wilson, Thomas E.   "Gulf Oil in Cabinda, " Africa Today, Vol. 17, No. 4, 1970, pp. 20-26.

World Bank Atlas: Population, Per Capita Product and Growth Rate. Washington, D. C.: The World Bank (annual).

VI. SCIENTIFIC

Amaral, Ilídio do. Ensaio de um Estudo Geográfico da Rede Urbana de Angola. Lisbon: Junta de Investigações do Ultramar, 1962.

_____. Luanda (Estudo de Geografia Urbana). Lisbon: Junta de Investigações do Ultramar, 1968.

Bebiano, José Bacellar. Geologia e Riqueza Mineira de Angola. Lisbon: Instituto Superior de Comércio, 1923.

Boléo, José de Oliveira. Ensaio sobre Geografia Agrária. Angola--a Terra e o Homem. Lisbon: Agência Geral do Ultramar, 1958.

Clement, A. J. "The Kunene River (Angola), " Geographical Magazine, Vol. 38, 1965, pp. 458-472.

O Clima de Angola. Luanda: Serviços Meteorológicos, 1955.

Ficalho, Conde de. Plantas Utéis da Africa Portuguesa. 2d edition. Lisbon: Agência Geral das Colónias, 1947.

Fleury, Ernest. Notes sur la Géologie et la Paléontologie de l'Angola. Lisbon: Instituto Superior de Comércio de Lisboa, 1923.

Garcia, J. G. Contribuições para o Conhecimento da Flora de Angola e de Moçambique. Lisbon: Junta de Investigações do Ultramar, 1959.

Health Under Attack. London: Committee for Freedom in Mozambique, Angola and Guinea. Topics No. 2, n. d.

Kuder, Manfred. Angola: Eine Geographische Soziale und Wirtschaffliche Landeskunde. Darmstadt: Wissenschaftlich--Buchgesellschaft, 1971.

149

May, Jacques M. "The Ecology of Malnutrition in Seven Countries of Southern Africa and in Portuguese Guinea, " Vol. 10, Studies in Medical Geography. New York: Hafner, 1971.

Medeiros, Carlos Alberto. A Colonização das Terras Altas da Huíla (Angola). Estudo de Geografia Humana. Lisbon: Centro de Estudos Geográficos, 1976.

Ribeiro, Henrique, and A. C. M. de Carvalho. "A Malaria Study at Luanda, Angola, " Anais do Instituto de Medicina Tropical, Vol. XXI, No. 1-2, January-June 1964, pp. 181-186.

_____, V. M. R. Casaca, and J. A. L. P. Cochofel. "A Malaria Survey in the Lobito-Catumbela Region, Angola, " Anais do Instituto de Medicina Tropical, Vol. XXI, No. 3-4, July-December 1964, pp. 337-352.

Shaw, H. K. Airy. "The Vegetation of Angola, " Journal of Ecology, Vol. XXXV, 1947, pp. 23-48.

Van Dongen, I. S. "Angola, " Focus (American Geographical Society), Vol. VII, No. 2, October 1956, pp. 1-6.

Whittlesey, D. S. "Geographic Provinces of Angola, " Geographical Review, Vol. XIV, No. 1, January 1974, pp. 113-126.

VII. SOCIAL

Anthropology

Almeida, António de. Bushmen and Other Non-Bantu Peoples of Angola: Three Lectures. Johannesburg: Witwatersrand University Press, 1965.

Cabrita, Carlos L. Antunes. Em Terras de Luenas, Breve Estudo Sobre os Usos e Costumes da Tribo Luena. Lisbon: Agência Geral do Ultramar, 1954.

Cerqueira, Ivo Benjamim de. Vida Social Indigena na Colónia de Angola (Usos e Costumes). Lisbon: Agência Geral das Colónias, 1947.

Chatelain, Heli. Folk Tales of Angola. Memoirs of the American Folklore Society, Boston, 1894.

Childs, G. M. Umbundu Kinship and Character. London: Oxford University Press, International African Institute, 1949.

Cruz, José Ribeiro da. Notas de Etnografia Angolana. Lisbon: n. p., 1940.

Delachaux, Theodore. Ethnographie de la Région du Cunene. Neuchatel: V. Attinger, 1948.

_____. Pays et Peuples d'Angola. Neuchatel: V. Attinger, 1934.

Denis, J. Les Yaka du Kwango. Tervuren: Musée Royale de l'Afrique Centrale, 1964.

Dinis, José de Oliveira Ferreira. Populações Indigenas de Angola. Coimbra: Imprensa da Universidade, 1918.

151

Edwards, Adrian C.   The Ovimbundu Under Two Sovereign-
   ties: A Study of Social Control and Social Change Among
   a People of Angola.   London: Oxford University Press,
   International African Institute, 1962.

Ennis, Merlin.   Umbundu Folk Tales from Angola.   Boston:
   Beacon, 1962.

Estermann, Carlos.   Etnografia do Sudoeste de Angola.   3
   vols.   Lisbon: Junta de Investigações do Ultramar, 1960-
   61.

_____.   A Vida Económica dos Bantos do Sudoeste de
   Angola.   Luanda: Junta Provincial de Povoamento de Angola, 1971.

Felgas, H. A. E.   As Populações Nativas do Norte de Angola.   Lisbon: N. p., 1965.

Gibson, Gordon D.   The Ethnography of Southwestern Angola.
   Vol. I: The Non-Bantu Peoples: The Ambo Ethnic Group.
   Vol. II: The Nyaneka-Nkumbi Ethnic Group.   New York:
   Africana, 1976 and 1979 (Trans. of Estermann, Ethno-
   grafia do Sudoeste de Angola, Vol. I).

Hambly, Wilfrid D.   The Ovimbundu of Angola.   Chicago:
   Field Museum of Natural History,   Anthropological Series,
   Vol. XXI, No. 2, 1934.

Hauenstein, Alfred.   Les Hanya: Description d'un Groupe
   Ethnique Bantou de l'Angola.   Wiesbaden: Steiner, 1967.

Henderson, Lawrence W.   "Ethno-Linguistic Worlds, " in
   Robert T. Parsons (ed.), Windows on Africa: A Symposium.   Leiden: E. J. Brill, 1971, pp. 50-60.

Lima, Mesquitela.   A Etnografia Angolana: Considerações
   Acerca da sua Problemática Actual.   Luanda: Museu de
   Angola, 1964.

_____.   Fonctions Sociologiques des Figurines de Culte
   Hamba dans la Société et dans la Culture Tshokwe (Angola).   Luanda: IICA, 1971.

McCulloch, Merran.   The Ovimbundu of Angola.   London:
   Oxford University Press, International African Institute,
   1952.

_____. The Southern Lunda and Related Peoples. London: Oxford University Press, International African Institute, 1951.

MacGaffey, Wyatt. Custom and Government in the Lower Congo. Berkeley and Los Angeles: University of California Press, 1970.

_____. "Kongo and the King of the Americas, " Journal of Modern African Studies, Vol. VI, No. 2, 1968, pp. 171-181.

Martins, Joaquim. Sabedoria Cabinda: Simbolos e Provérbios. Lisbon: Junta de Investigações do Ultramar, 1968.

Martins, M. A. Morais. Contactos de Culturas no Congo Português. Lisbon: Junta de Investigações do Ultramar, 1958.

Matta, J. D. Cordeiro da. Philosophia Popular em Provérbios Angolenses. Lisbon: Typographia e Stereotypia Moderna, 1891.

Milheiros, Mário. Notas de Etnografia Angolana. Luanda: IICA, 1967.

Plancquaert, M. Les Jaga et les Bayaka du Kwango. Brussels: Mémo., Institut Royal Colonial Belge, 1932.

Redinha, José. Distribuição Etnica da Província de Angola. Luanda: Centro de Informação e Turismo de Angola, 1962.

_____. Etnosociologia do Nordeste de Angola. Braga: Editôra Pax, 1966.

Van Wing, J. Etudes Bakongo. 2 vols. 2d edition. Brussels: Desclée de Brouwer, 1959.

Vaz, José Martins. No Mundo Dos Cabindas: Estudo Etnográfico. 2 vols. Lisbon: Editorial LIAM, 1970.

Weeks, J. H. "Notes on Some Customs of the Lower Congo People, " Folklore, Vol. XIX, No. 4, 1908, pp. 409-437.

Demography

Amaral, Ilídio do. Aspectos do Povoamento Branco de Angola. Lisbon: Junta de Investigações do Ultramar, 1960.

Bender, Gerald J., and P. Stanley Yoder. "Whites in Angola on the Eve of Independence: The Politics of Numbers, " Africa Today, Vol. XXI, No. 4, 1974, pp. 23-37.

Francis, Donald. "The Demography of the Portuguese Territories: Angola, Mozambique and Portuguese Guinea, " in W. I. Brass, et al. (eds.), The Demography of Tropical Africa. Princeton: Princeton University Press, 1968, pp. 440-465.

Morgado, Nuno Alves. Aspectos da Evolução Demográfica da População da Antiga Província do Congo, 1949-1956. Lisbon: Junta de Investigações do Ultramar, 1959.

Pélissier, René. "Conséquences Démographiques des Révoltes en Afrique Portugaise (1961-1970): Essai d'Interpretation, " Revue Française d'Histoire d'Outre-Mer, Vol. LXI, No. 222, 1974, pp. 47-64.

Província de Angola. 3º Recenseamento Geral da População, 1960. Vol. I-IV and annex. Luanda: 1964 and 1967.

Education

Clignet, Remi. "Inadequacies of the Notion of Assimilation in African Education, " Journal of Modern African Studies, Vol. 8, October 1970, pp. 425-444.

Heimer, Franz-Wilhelm. Educação e Sociedade nas Areas Rurais de Angola: Resultados de um Inquérito. Volumes 1, 2, 3. Luanda: Missão de Inquéritos Agrícolas de Angola, 1972-74.

_____. "Education, Economics and Social Change in Rural Angola: The Case of the Cuima Region, " in F. W. Heimer (ed.), Social Change in Angola. Munich: Weltforum Verlag, pp. 111-144.

Liberation Through Learning. London: Committee for Freedom in Mozambique, Angola and Guinea. Topics No. 4, n. d.

Lisboa, Eugenio A.   "Education in Angola and Mozambique, "
in B. Rose (ed.), Education in Southern Africa. London:
Collier-Macmillan, 1970, pp. 264-321.

Margarido, Alfredo.   "L'Enseignement en Afrique dite Portugaise, " Revue Française d'Etudes Politiques Africaines,
No. 56, August 1970, pp. 62-85.

Mondlane, Eduardo and Janet.   "Portuguese Africa, " in
Helen Kitchen (ed.), The Educated African. New York:
Praeger, 1962, pp. 235-245.

Província de Angola.   Direcção Provincial dos Serviços de
Estatística. Estatística de Educação (annual).

Samuels, Michael A.   Education in Angola 1878-1914. A
History of Culture Transfer and Administration. New
York: Teachers' College Press, Columbia University,
1970.

_____. "A Failure of Hope: Education and Changing Op-
portunities in Angola Under the Portuguese Republic, " in
Ronald H. Chilcote, Protest and Resistance in Angola and
Brazil. Berkeley: University of California Press, 1972,
pp. 53-66.

_____. "The 'New Look' in Angolan Education, " Africa
Report, Vol. 12, No. 8, November 1967, pp. 63-66.

_____, and Norman A. Bailey.   "Education, Health, and
Social Welfare, " in D. M. Abshire and M. A. Samuels
(eds.), Portuguese Africa: A Handbook. New York:
Praeger, 1969, pp. 178-201.

Santos, Martins dos.   História do Ensino em Angola. Luanda: Edição dos Serviços de Educação, 1970.

Scalon, M. A. D.   "Methodist Education in Angola, 1897-
1915, " Studia, No. 20-22, April-December 1967, pp. 75-
107.

Silva, E. M. da.   "Social Conditions of School Attendance
and Achievement of Minors in Suburban Luanda: A Preliminary Test of Some Hypotheses, " in F. W. Heimer
(ed.), Social Change in Angola. Munich: Weltforum Verlag, pp. 194-210.

Religion

Andersson, Efraim.   Messianic Popular Movements in the
Lower Congo.   Uppsala: Almquist & Wiksells, 1958.

Baptist Missionary Society.   1878-1978:   One Hundred Years
of Christian Mission in Angola and Zaire.   London: Baptist Missionary Society, 1978.

Barrett, D. B.   Schism and Renewal in Africa.   Nairobi:
Oxford University Press, 1968.

Costa, Cândido F. da.   Cem Anos dos Missionários do Espírito Santo em Angola, 1866-1966.   Nova Lisboa: N. p.,
1970.

Cunha, M. Alves da.   Missões Católicas de Angola.   Luanda:
Imprensa Nacional da Colónia de Angola, n. d.

Henderson, Lawrence W.   "Protestantism: A Tribal Religion, " in Robert T. Parsons (ed.), Windows on Africa:
A Symposium.   Leiden: E. J. Brill, 1971, pp. 61-80.

Janzen, John M. , and Wyatt MacGaffey.   An Anthology of
Kongo Religion: Primary Texts from Lower Zaire.
Lawrence: University of Kansas, Publications in Anthropology, 5, 1974.

MacGaffey, Wyatt.   "Comparative Analysis of Central African
Religions, " Africa, Vol. 42, No. 1, 1972, pp. 21-31.

_____. "Cultural Roots of Kongo Prophetism, " History of
Religions, Vol. 17, No. 2, November 1977, pp. 177-193.

Margarido, Alfredo.   "The Tokoist Church and Portuguese
Colonialism in Angola, " in Ronald H. Chilcote, Protest
and Resistance in Angola and Brazil.   Berkeley: University of California Press, 1972, pp. 29-52.

Okuma, Thomas.   "The Social Response of Christianity in
Angola: Selected Issues, " unpublished Ph. D. dissertation.
School of Theology, Boston University, 1964.

Ranger, T. O.   "Territorial Cults in the History of Central
Africa, " Journal of African History, 1973, Vol. XIV, pp.
581-597.

Ribas, Oscar. Iludo, Divinidades e Ritos Angolanos. Luanda: Museu de Angola, 1958. (Second edition: IICA, 1975.)

Santos, Eduardo do. Movimentos Proféticos e Mágicos em Angola. Lisbon: Imprensa Nacional, 1972.

Soremekun, F. "A History of the American Board Missions in Angola, 1880-1940, " unpublished Ph. D. dissertation. Northwestern University, 1965.

_____ . "Religion and Politics in Angola: The American Board Missions and the Portuguese Government, 1880-1922, " Cahiers d'Etudes Africaine, Vol. II, No. 43, 1971, pp. 341-377.

Tucker, John T. Angola: The Land of the Blacksmith Prince. London: World Dominion Press, 1933.

Sociology

Batacha, Fernando. A Urbanização de Angola. Luanda: Museu de Angola, 1950.

Bender, Gerald J. "Planned Rural Settlements in Angola, 1900-1968, " in F. W. Heimer (ed.), Social Change in Angola. Munich: Weltforum Verlag, 1973, pp. 236-279.

Carvalho, E. C. de. "Esboço da Zonagem Agrícola de Angola, " Fomento, Vol. I, No. 3, 1963, pp. 67-72.

_____ . " 'Traditional' and 'Modern' Patterns of Cattle Raising in South-Western Angola: A Critical Evaluation of Change from Pastoralism to Ranching, " Journal of Developing Areas, January 8, 1974, pp. 199-226.

_____ , and J. V. da Silva. "The Cunene Region: Ecological Analysis of an African Agropastoral System, " in F. W. Heimer, Social Change in Angola. Munich: Weltforum Verlag, 1973, pp. 146-192.

Heimer, Franz-Wilhelm (ed.). Social Change in Angola. Munich: Weltforum Verlag, 1973.

Monteiro, Ramis Ladeiro. A Família nos Musseques de Luanda. Luanda: Fundo de Assistência Social no Trabalho, 1973.

_____ . "From Extended to Residual Family: Aspects of Social Change in the Musseques of Luanda, " in F. W. Heimer (ed.), Social Change in Angola. Munich: Weltforum Verlag, 1973, pp. 211-234.

Niddrie, David L. "Changing Settlement Patterns in Angola, " Rural Africana, Vol. 23, 1974, pp. 47-77.

_____ . "Some Recent Settlement Schemes in Angola, " Journal of the American Portuguese Cultural Society, Vol. I, 1967, pp. 25-31.

Possinger, H. "Interrelations Between Economic and Social Change in Rural Africa: The Case of the Ovimbundu of Angola, " in F. W. Heimer (ed.), Social Change in Angola. Munich: Weltforum Verlag, 1973, pp. 32-52.

Silva, J. V. da, and J. A. de Morais. "Ecological Conditions of Social Change in the Central Highlands of Angola, " in F. W. Heimer (ed.), Social Change in Angola. Munich: Weltforum Verlag, 1973, pp. 94-109.

Strangeway, A. K. "The Advance of African Women in Angola, " African Women, Vol. I, No. 4, June 1956.

Urquhart, Alvin W. Patterns of Settlement and Subsistence in South-western Angola. Washington, D. C.: National Research Council, Publication 1096, 1963.

VIII. CULTURAL

Archaeology

Clark, J. Desmond. Further Paleo-Anthropological Studies
in Northern Lunda. Lisbon: Companhia de Diamantes de
Angola, Serviços Culturais, 1968.

_____. Prehistoric Cultures of Northeast Angola and
their Significance in Tropical Africa. 2 vols. Lisbon:
Companhia de Diamantes de Angola, Serviços Culturais,
1963.

Gibson, Gordon D., and J. E. Yellen. "A Middle Stone Age
Assemblage from the Munhiro Mission, Huila District,
Angola, " South African Archaeological Bulletin, Vol.
XXXIII, 1978, pp. 76-83.

Janmark, J. La Station Préhistorique de Candala District
de la Lunda. Lisbon: Companhia de Diamantes de Angola, Serviços Culturais, No. 2, 1948.

_____. Stations Préhistoriques de l'Angola du Nord-Est.
Lisbon: Companhia de Diamantes de Angola, Serviços
Culturais, No. 1, 1947.

Leakey, L. S. B. Tentative Study of the Pleistocene Climatic Changes and Stone Age Culture Sequence in Northeastern Angola. Lisbon: Companhia de Diamantes de
Angola, Serviços Culturais, No. 4, 1949.

Maret, P. de, F. van Noten, and D. Cahen. "Radiocarbon
Dates from West Central Africa, " Journal of African History, Vol. XVIII, No. 4, 1977, pp. 481-505.

159

Art and Music

Adelman, Kenneth Lee.   "The Art of the Yaka, " African
Arts, Vol. IX, No. 1, October 1975, pp. 40-43.

Almeida, A. de.   "Tipos de Vestuário e Adornos de Alguns
Povos Bantos de Angola, " Garcia de Orta, Vol. III, No.
2, 1955, pp. 213-216.

Bastin, Marie-Louise.   Art Decoratif Tshokwe.   2 vols.
Lisbon: Companhia de Diamantes de Angola, Serviços
Culturais, 1961.

_____. "Arts of the Angolan Peoples. I: Tshokwe, "
African Arts, Vol. II, No. 1, 1968, pp. 40-46, 60-64.

_____. "Arts of the Angolan Peoples. II: Lwena, "
African Arts, Vol. II, No. 2, 1969, pp. 46-53, 77-80.

_____. "Arts of the Angolan Peoples. III: Songo, "
African Arts, Vol. II, No. 3, 1969, pp. 51-57, 77-81.

_____. "Arts of the Angolan Peoples. IV: Mbundu, "
African Arts, Vol. II, No. 4, 1969, pp. 30-37, 74-76.

_____. "Les Styles de la Sculpture Tshokwe, " Arts d'Af-
rique Noire, Vol. 19, Autumn 1976, pp. 16-35.

Batalha, Fernando.   A Arquitectura Tradicional de Luanda.
Luanda: Museu de Angola, 1950.

Baumann, Hermann.   "Angola, " in Encyclopaedia of World
Art, Vol. I. New York: McGraw-Hill, 1959, pp. 463-
466.

Folclore Musical de Angola.   Angola Folk Music: Collection
of Magnetic Tapes and Discs. 2 vols. Lisbon: Companhia de Diamantes de Angola, Serviços Culturais, 1967.

Gibson, Gordon D. , and Cecilia R. McGurk.   "High-Status
Caps of the Kongo and Mbundu Peoples, " Textile Museum
Journal, Vol. IV, 1977, pp. 71-96.

Hauenstein, A.   "La Poterie chez les Ovimbundu (Angola), "
Acta tropica, Vol. XXI, No. 1, 1964, pp. 48-81.

Kubik, Gerhard.   Musica Tradicional e Aculturada dos ! Kung
de Angola. Lisbon: Junta de Investigações do Ultramar, 1970.

_____. Naturesa e a Stratura de Escalas Musicaes Africanas. Lisbon: Junta de Investigações do Ultramar, 1970.

Redinha, José. Máscaras de Madeira do Lunda e Alto Zambeze. Lisbon: Companhia de Diamantes de Angola, Publicações Culturais, 1956.

_____. Paredes Pintadas da Lunda. Lisbon: Companhia de Diamantes de Angola, Publicações Culturais, No. 1, 1946.

Söderberg, B. Les Instruments de Musique au Bas-Congo et dans les Régions Avoisinantes. Stockholm: Ethographical Museum of Sweden, 1956.

Wannyn, R. L. L'Art Ancien du Metal au Bas Congo. Champles par Wavre, Belgium: Editions du Vieux Planquesauie, 1961.

Linguistics

Alves, P. Albino. Dicionário etimológico Bundo-Português. 2 vols. Lisbon: Tip. Silvas, 1951.

Assis Júnior, António de. Dicionário Kimbundu-Português. Luanda: Argente, Santos, n. d.

Atkins, Guy. "A Demographic Survey of the Kimbundu-Kongo Language Border in Angola, " Boletim da Sociedade de Geografia de Lisboa, Vol. LXXIII, No. 7-9, 1955, pp. 325-347.

_____. "An Outline of Hungu Grammar," Garcia de Orta (Lisbon), Vol. II, No. 2, 1954, pp. 145-164.

Bentley, W. H. Dictionary and Grammar of the Kongo language as spoken at San Salvador. 2 vols. London: Baptist Missionary Society, Trubner, 1887-1895.

Chatelain, Héli. Grammatica Elementar de Kimbundo ou Língua de Angola. Geneva: Typ. de C. Schuchardt, 1888-1889.

Dalby, David (ed.). Language and History in Africa. New York: Africana, 1970.

Greenberg, Joseph. "Linguistic Evidence Regarding Bantu Origins, " Journal of African History, Vol. XIII, No. 2, 1972, pp. 189-216.

Guthrie, Malcolm. Comparative Bantu: An Introduction to the Comparative Linguistics and Prehistory of the Bantu Languages. 4 vols. Farnborough: Gregg Press, 1967-72.

Magalhães, António Miranda. Manual de Línguas Indigenas de Angola. Luanda: Imprensa Nacional de Angola, 1922.

Nascimento, J. Pereira do. Diccionário Portuguez-Kimbundu. Huíla: Typographia da Missão, 1903.

_____. Grammática do Umbundu, ou Língua de Benguella. Lisbon: Imprensa Nacional, 1894.

Tavares, José Lourenço. "Línguas e Dialectos Bantu de Angola, " Congresso do Mundo Português, Vol. XIV, 1940, pp. 461-510.

Valente, Padre José Francisco. Gramática Umbundu, A Língua do Centro de Angola. Lisbon: Junta de Investigações do Ultramar, 1966.

Literature

Whilst several anthologies of poetry from Angola have been translated into English, there are few Angolan novels available in English. Only some of the main works are cited here. Other titles can be found in the bibliographies of the books by Hamilton and Moser.

Andrade, Mário de (ed.). Antologia da Poesia Negra de Expressão Portuguesa. Paris: P. J. Oswald, 1958.

_____. Literatura Africana de Expressão Portuguesa. Vol. I: Poesia. Antologia Temática. Algiers, 1967; Vol. II: Prosa. Algiers, 1968. Both reprinted, Liechtenstein: Kraus Reprint, 1970.

_____. "Literature and Nationalism in Angola, " Présence Africaine, Vol. XIII, No. 41, 1962, pp. 115-122.

Antonio, Mário. Luanda "Ilha" Crioula. Lisbon: Agência Geral do Ultramar, 1968.

_____ . 100 poemas. Luanda: ABC, 1963.

_____ . A Sociedade Angolana do Fim do Século XIX e um seu Escritor. Luanda: Nos, 1961.

Assis Júnior, António de. O Segredo da Morta. Luanda: A. Luzitana, 1934.

Bastide, Roger. L'Afrique dans l'Oeuvre de Castro Soromenho. Paris: P. J. Oswald, 1960.

Burness, Donald. Fire: Six Writers from Angola, Mozambique and Cape Verde. Washington, D. C.: Three Continents Press, 1977.

Costa, Andrade. "Two Expressions of Angolanity, " Présence Africaine, Vol. XIV-XV, 1962, pp. 42-43, 70-84.

Cruz, Viriato da. "Responsibilities of the Negro Intellectual, " Présence Africaine, No. 27-28, August-November 1959, pp. 321-339.

Cultura. 1945-51, 1957-61. (A scientific, literary and artistic news journal.)

Dickinson, Margaret (ed.). When Bullets Begin to Flower: Poems of Resistance from Angola, Mozambique and Guinea. Nairobi: East African Publishing House, 1972.

Hamilton, Russell G. Voices from an Empire: A History of Afro-Portuguese Literature. Minneapolis: University of Minnesota Press, 1975.

Holness, Malga. "The Poetry of Agostinho Neto, " Afriscope, Vol. V, No. 5, 1975, pp. 32-40.

Hughes, Heather. "Protest Poetry in Pre-Independence Mozambique and Angola, " English in Africa, Vol. 4, March 1977, pp. 18-31.

Margarido, Alfredo (ed.). Poetas Angolanas. Lisbon: Casa dos Estudantes do Império, 1962.

_____ . "The Social and Economic Background of Portuguese Negro Poetry, " Diogenes, Vol. 37, Spring 1962, pp. 50-74.

Mensagem.   1951-52.   (A literary-cultural review.)

Moser, Gerald M.   "African Literature in the Portuguese
Language, " Journal of General Education, Vol. XIII, No.
4, January 1962, pp. 270-304.

_____.   "African Literature in Portuguese: The First
Written, the Last Discovered, " African Forum, Vol. II,
No. 4, Spring 1967, pp. 78-96.

_____.   Essays in Portuguese-African Literature.   Uni-
versity Park: Pennsylvania State University Studies, No.
26, 1969.

_____.   A Tentative Portuguese-African Bibliography:
Portuguese Literature in Africa and African Literature in
the Portuguese Language.   University Park: Pennsylvania
State University Libraries, 1970.

Neto, A. , M. Andrade, and M. Ollivier.   Sacred Hope.   Dar
es Salaam: Tanzania Publishing House, 1974.

Neto, Agostinho.   Poemas.   Lisbon: Casa dos Estudantes
do Império, 1961.

Preto-Rodas, Richard A.   Négritude as a Theme in the Po-
etry of the Portuguese-Speaking World.   University of
Florida Humanities Monograph No. 31.   Gainesville:
University of Florida Press, 1970.

Ribas, Oscar.   Nuvens que passam.   Luanda: Author, 1927.

_____.   O Resgate de Uma Falta.   Luanda: Author, 1929.

Soromenho, Castro.   Homens Sem Caminho.   Lisbon: Portu-
gália, 1942.

_____.   Sertanejos de Angola.   Lisbon: Agência Geral
das Colónias, 1943.

_____.   Terras Mortas.   Rio de Janeiro: Celecção Gav-
ista, 1949.

Vieira, José Luandino.   A Cidade e a Infância.   Lisbon:
Casa dos Estudantes do Império, 1960.

_____.   Luuanda.   Belo Horizonte: Editora Eros, 1965.

_____. The Real Life of Domingos Xavier. (Translated by Michael Wolfers.) London: Heinemann, African Writers Series, 1978.

_____. Vidas Novas. Porto: Afrontamento, 1975.

INDEX